Architectural production has been rather unsuccessful at keeping up with technological advances. The inertia of a building industry that for the most part employs century-old technologies, a property market which avoids risk (and thus often innovation) and the weight of historic and semantic considerations in the evolution of the discipline have been determining factors in architecture's sluggishness when compared to the progress made by other design-related practices, such as the automobile and aeronautical industries. In fact, as computer-aided design invaded all these practices in the 1980s, radically transforming their generative foundations and productive capacities, architecture found itself most out-of-step and least alert, immersed in ideological and tautological debates and adrift in a realm of referents severed from material production.

Therefore it is not surprising that the first significant impact of computer applications on architectural design would have more to do with formal and stylistic research (as it was with a large part of post-modern scenographic investigation) than with any exploitation of the capacity of the new technologies for redefining the way architecture might be conceived of and produced in response to the fundamental link established between information and matter.

Today, the long-running experimental and formative task carried out at several (and ever more numerous) academic institutions and the widespread perception of the benefits of technological innovation to our everyday environment have contributed to the definition of a new (less stable, more intimate) relation between technology and architectural production. This is the new reality that the boogazine *Verb* and especially *Verb Natures* —which this monograph complements— have sought to encourage and expand.

In this new production context, increasing importance has been given to the role of parametric design, a process based not on fixed metric quantities but on consistent relationships between objects, allowing changes in a single element to propagate corresponding changes throughout the system. In parallel, developments in scripting have opened the way to algorithmic design processes that allow complex forms to be grown from simple iterative methods while preserving specified qualities. If the parametric is a technique for the holistic control and manipulation of design objects at all scales from part to whole, the algorithmic is a method of generation, producing complex forms and structures based on simple component rules.

Through complementary approaches from the fields of architecture and engineering, *From Control to Design* presents a series of experiments (linked to projects published in *Verb* and other recent Actar publications) that show how innovation in the modelling and fabrication processes facilitate a link between the realms of formal research and production, with a growing capacity for control over project implementation and materialization, over the optimization of resources, over execution times and over a substantial improvement in building quality.

Michael Meredith

is Associate Professor of Architecture at the Harvard Graduate
School of Design and the co-director with Hilary Sample of MOS,
an interdisciplinary practice focusing on architecture and design
through research and the production of multivalent architectural
objects. The work engages issues ranging from typology, digital
methodologies, the physical context of structure, fabrication,
materiality, tactility, and use; to the larger social, cultural, and
environmental networks. **www.mos-office.net**

Yes, we use parametric modeling, but so what. Like others, we're drawn towards totalizing systems of organization versatile enough to engage variable relationships, diverse parameters and complex proportions. (That said, there is no purely scalar relational organization, absolute measure can never be avoided when dealing with architecture due to material constraints, building codes, and the anthropomorphic imperatives of architecture.)

Recently, in the disciplinary attempts to utilize the power of the parametric process it seems as if everyone awoke from the embarrassing drunken party of post-modernism, trying to forget everything that happened.

Never enough
(transform, repeat ad nausea)

The architectural field's current use of the parametric has been superficial and skin-deep, maybe importantly so, lacking of a larger framework of referents, narratives, history, and forces. Despite the contemporary collective desire to forget postmodern semiotic signification, everything visual eventually devolves into symbolic imagery. The recent architectural production has been dedicated towards a post-post-modern architecture of radical distortion as a way to escape signification and subvert semiotic legibility (twisted hyperbolic forms, stretched out shapes, extreme continuity of planes and surfaces, etc.). I would argue that the "parametric work" being produced today fits within an evolution of so-called postmodernism, concerning the image and referent although the parametric is the tautological modulated image of quantity; the indexical referent is itself and analogous systems. To the extent the profession has utilized parametrics today, there is very little instigating complexity other than a mind-numbing image of complexity, falling far short of its rich potential to correlate multivalent processes or typological transformations, parallel meanings, complex functional requirements, site-specific problems or collaborative networks. When some-thing supposedly looks "parametric" today, it's aesthetic (re)production—the repeti-tion of quality and taste. The mastering of hi-tech engineering software is ultimately used to produce ornate architectural decoration. The escape of referents through radical distortion becomes just another referent, albeit a solipsistic one.

Due to the inherent specificity of computational complexity or the desire for visual unifying consistency, parametric design typically reduces the number of formal variables, but maximizes their variability through transformational affects which are engendered via quantity. Although, this is extremely pragmatic in the produc-tion of panelized doubly curved surfaces (which is how we've used it in the temporary Huyghe puppet theater project and the Drive-in screen, ground, projection booth) it can quickly devolve into an aesthetic solely based upon the transformation of parts within a field, a totalizing smooth and singular formal aesthetic. The parametric is a totalizing aesthetic built upon the legacy of American formalism, an ideology which has since transformed from an important critique of functionalist dogma as a positivist and naively utopian discourse into its own positivist position ("it has to be that way because of the geometry or form" or "the software did it").

Parametric design fits within an architectural discipline that is simultaneously searching for a unified organizational clarity (the diagram, parti, etc.) and visual complexity (Venturi), but no matter how patterned, totalizing and parametric it is, architecture is inevitably a fragment, a disfigured orphaned object, even if it is a field or in a field. It requires differentiation for it to become Architectural, and it is the socio-political that allows it to escape the emptiness of objects. Architecture requires social engagement; it requires cultural/social relevance. It is not the parametric, the relentlessness malleability of form, nor is it complexity for its own sake, but rather a complex of complex relationships that produce architecture. The operational para-digm we're interested in is akin to Pierre Bourdieau's "field of cultural production," where form is the playing field within competing vectors within a larger cultural field of forces (instead of internalized language games). The specificity and agency of architecture can only happen within the particulars of its situation and in relation to the larger field. Architectural production is no longer the Marxist "us vs. them" dialectical model of resistance. In architecture there is only criticism within the market culture and something can only become critical in relation to things outside itself. Similarly, I've always considered the dialectical opposition of form vs. material, at the least, exaggerated. It's an opposition born of post-modernist signification, where form is more critical/meaningful to signification than material in which the form is based. This distinction is too simplistic and dogmatic. The potential of complex parametric relationships are to become radically inclusive and reconcile this artificial, form-vs.-material binary. Parametric models offer another type of play and design process based around multiplicity of scalar parameters, but it never resolves what parameters are necessary for architecture.

Like the other architects in this book, we're guilty as charged—formalists, specifically interested in fields of formal relationships. For us, the persistent architectural narrative of formalism has evolved so that the specificity of use is more important than the instantiation of form for its own sake. However, the instantiation of "use" should not be misconstrued as a simply pragmatic or functionalist narrative, but rather as against the simplistic and totalizing solipsistic internalization of architectural production. Use is about the performance of architecture: the double *entendre* of performance, both of utility and theatrical value/relevance.

Today, disciplinary formal games (unlike in the 80s and early 90s) need a purpose other than aesthetic experimentation in itself. The architecture discipline—the academy's legacy of beaux-arts formalism—has become so watered down and vague that it no longer provides a strong armature to work against or within. Without a broader system, the drive for form has been listless, lost in self-referential exercises, meaningless outside the field of architecture itself. Instead, architecture should *perform* rather than simply *form;* structurally, environmentally, economically, programmatically, contextually, or in multiple formal arenas. Formal distortions need to have purpose or cultural relevance and cannot stand alone as games or algorithms. Within this new discourse, meaning can be constructed locally and relationally.

The discourse of architecture has been too bound up in the techniques of its own construction, not its cultural social situation. Of course technique is part of the cultural situation, but we've forgotten about everything else. The object of architecture has become so depoliticized and neutered that we think it's just a progression of different tribal ideologies. Ideology is personalized to the point where there is almost no discourse. Performance optimization is not a fundamental architectural problem. Architecture is primarily a cultural socio-political form, not technological determinism; it's super vague, it's inclusive, relational, it's parametric, but it's far more complex than any of us could singularly map out within the computer and totally understand because it's out of our grasp. Not everything is easily quantifiable not all relationships are geometric and not all are to be coordinated into a smooth relationship.

Traditionally the enemy of avant-garde art and architecture is the production of taste and quality, false expression of the culture. We are not against these *per se*, but operating without an apriori "style" means we are looking to define an alternate quality, one that is specific to its situation, one that establishes an alternate space for itself within its site. It doesn't have to express a generalized sense of culture, but the cultural variables that are at play within the specific situation. What is interesting to us is within the armature of each project, looking for new methods for the production of work, utilizing parametrics, but also establishing another mode of working in our office that isn't based upon traditional "top-down" hierarchical structures. The quality of the work depends on the depth of meaning generated by the specific circumstances/parameters of the cultural landscape it occupies; in this, the parametric can engage its full capacities.

Ultimately, what interests us about the parametric project is exactly what it excludes, the socio-political dimension of architecture. Parametrics' potential is to produce a hyperinclusive network of parameters and relationships—the more multivalent the object the more meaningful and complex it is. The more multivalent the object the more engaged it is in culture/market and the more elusive it is to being absorbed by it. At the very least, the narrative of "use" provides some sort of agency to form making, deriving meaning through the influence and production of formal contingencies—variable relationships from inside and outside the architectural object. Constructing use as the performance of architecture, however, is not about reconstituting a neo-neo-function-alism or a post-post-functionalism, it is against the dialectical opposition (function-alism/formalism) of form follows function. Use is a narrative structure. Constructing narratives of utility provides an escape from a tautological parametric solipsism without forsaking formalism by providing an instrumentality of form, which could include pragmatic performance, the visceral, as well as the intellectual, discursive, or meaningful. The potential for use is synthesizing multiple narratives of architecture, typology (especially typology), performance, material, relational participation/produc-tion within a given site rather than autonomous legibility of internal relationships. These cultural, social, formal narratives provide architectural value. Use renders form as something more than an isolated physical or aesthetic object; it provides the archi-tectural object with both denotations and connotations which can resound outside an internalized field of signification. Through narratives of use, meaning is intimate, at a small scale and in relation to the specificity of its situation.

How has all of this affected our design process? I'm not exactly sure. (Within para-metric terms, typically, our projects are manifested through point fields that are easily manipulated through lines and their position on lines. Those lines are manipulated through surfaces, typically surface normals. Parameters are constructed; some rela-tionships are formalized while others remain immutable, due to constraints arising from site, material or structure. There is a clear hierarchy of elements and technique. Recently, we have been able to change this operative system where lines are produced through points that are produced through lines, and surfaces are produced through points or lines; essentially the hierarchy can break down and through scripting and programming within a parametric environment, through self-reflexive systems, the process can produce a sort of feedback loop of parameters.) We script, utilize and play with software in our work, and we appreciate the level of control and precision it offers, along with the intensive potential to experiment within a highly controlled environment. It is not all we do, but it is important to establish inclusive organizational systems. If anything an inclusive parametric process changes *how* we work, as well as our relationship to the 'office' itself. Parametric modeling is a discourse built upon techniques of either subdivision and/or aggregation (the perimeter is always arbitrary), but just as important are the office-laboratory, or workplace itself, as are the clients and users. The "apparatus" we use shifts and changes for each project. As Paolo Virno describes in his essay *Grammar of the Multitude*, the office is not a single person, nor is it a "we." Our office is a multitude of individuals and ideologies; there is no inside and outside; no "us" or "them;" inclusive of everything, excluding nothing. Everything can be internalized as a parameter. Our office itself is "parametric," a network of parameters connected to other offices and other fields, constructed of individuated opinions and persons that try to remain as open as possible. The system's openness is perhaps a direct result of the lack of a dominant ideology or position, certain aspects of an "open work," to use Umberto Eco's term. It describes one facet of current production, encouraging multiple readings, and the lack of any singular narrative, without a narrative hierarchy, where we look for "fields of meaning," instead of linear threads of meaning. As a result of this fluid system, the relationships that engage successive projects can shift or expand, constantly adapting to changes in the field, as well as socio-culture at large.

If our office is both an enactor of and an allegory for parametric systems, then the projects created within them are perhaps not as significant for their own sake as designs, but rather what they indicate about the evolving, if somewhat disoriented, nature of the field today. As specific (parametric) techniques of production and formal experimentation reveal the fluid normative workings within and between architectural offices, they also suggest how, in their (currently) problematic, proliferative and imagistic nature, context and use can be embedded in ever-multiplying, self-referential, parametric projects. However rudimentary the ways in which our offices are simultaneously and (albeit often unconsciously) cooperatively working to broaden and complexify formal experimentation, in order to imbue our technological development and their resultants with a socially grounded context, their very multiplicity and corresponding ambiguity can be extruded in such a way that the discipline of architecture itself, through the interaction between aforesaid "parametric" offices, possesses the potential to become a kind of ground-zero for the socio-political dimension currently missing from the current formalist trope of parametric modeling.

At the moment, we don't have any dominant prescriptive system, we consciously work within a very makeshift interdisciplinary practice engaging new media and methods of production, so parametric modeling truly helps us play by incorporating as many parameters as we can. Again, yes, the future is parametric, I have no doubt it will be, but technology won't fix all our problems; unfortunately, they're much deeper and much more human. Architecture can only be critical or difficult or meaningful or complex if it directly engages culture, if it becomes meaningful to a social cultural network. It can only persist if it is elusive. Parametric relational constructions have the capacity to become more inclusive, more adaptable, less absolutist... allowing for a new model that is not built upon the persistent dialectical constructions of form/function, but more inclusive more adaptable more socially relevant providing a provisional utopia, one that is here and now.

Puppet Theater

The theater was built in collaboration with the artist Pierre Huyghe, to house a puppet performance on the occasion of the 40th anniversary of the Carpenter Center. The design operates within the typical constraints of the typological theater—raked seating, acoustics, and unobstructed viewing—and uses parametric processes to create a theater that is suited to the unique conditions of the site.

In its relationship to the site, the theater appears as a foreign object occupying the Carpenter Center. The theater itself, rendered as a thin shell of moss-covered polycarbonate, appears disembodied from the typical poched enclosure of a theater, and reinstalled at the Carpenter Center: an organ placed in a new host. This dissonance of adjacencies is reinforced by the material choices; the green organic quality of the moss is supported by the glossy white polycarbonate structure. The moss-covering also serves as acoustical insulation to isolate noise from the busy street just a few feet from the theater.

0   10   30 FT

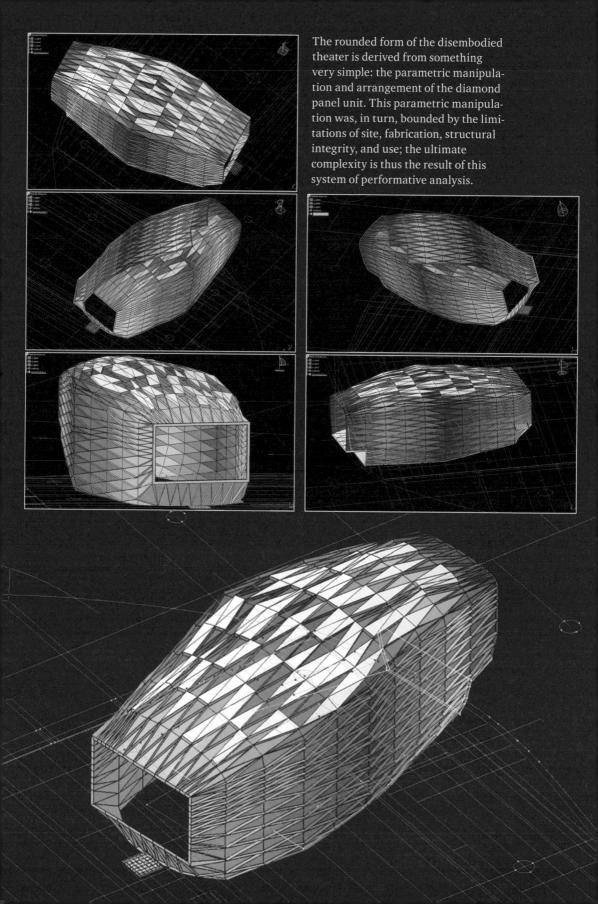

The rounded form of the disembodied theater is derived from something very simple: the parametric manipulation and arrangement of the diamond panel unit. This parametric manipulation was, in turn, bounded by the limitations of site, fabrication, structural integrity, and use; the ultimate complexity is thus the result of this system of performative analysis.

As a parameter, the site challenged the project through its unique context: Le Corbusier's Carpenter Center. The first parameter was set by the change in grade: the theater was set in a sunken patio, made inaccessible by a wall marking the four foot change in grade from street level. As a result, the rake of the seating relates to this grade change. Also, to avoid damaging the Carpenter Center, the envelope of the theater had to be independent of contact with the building's structural supports or ceiling overhead. Thus, navigating around the existing column grid of the Carpenter Center became an important parameter.

The unique condition of building a theater at the Carpenter Center also impacted fabrication. To avoid damaging the building, much of the theater was pre-fabricated off-site and assembled on-site using simple tools. Each of the 500 panels was fabricated as flat sheet of polycarbonate, which could then be folded to create the points of fastening to one another. The entire structure, in turn, could be assembled with the use of simple tools. All components were optimized for fabrication, transportation, and assembly of the finished theater. At the end of the puppet show's run, it was important that the theater could not only be disassembled, but would leave no permanent trace on the Carpenter Center. In addition to parameters of fabrication and assembly, the panels also perform structurally. Each panel was stiffened with foam inserts for rigidity, and strategic panels were turned inside-out to serve as keystones. Once assembled, the arrangement of panels dissipates force across the surface of the theater, forming a self-supporting monocoque skin.

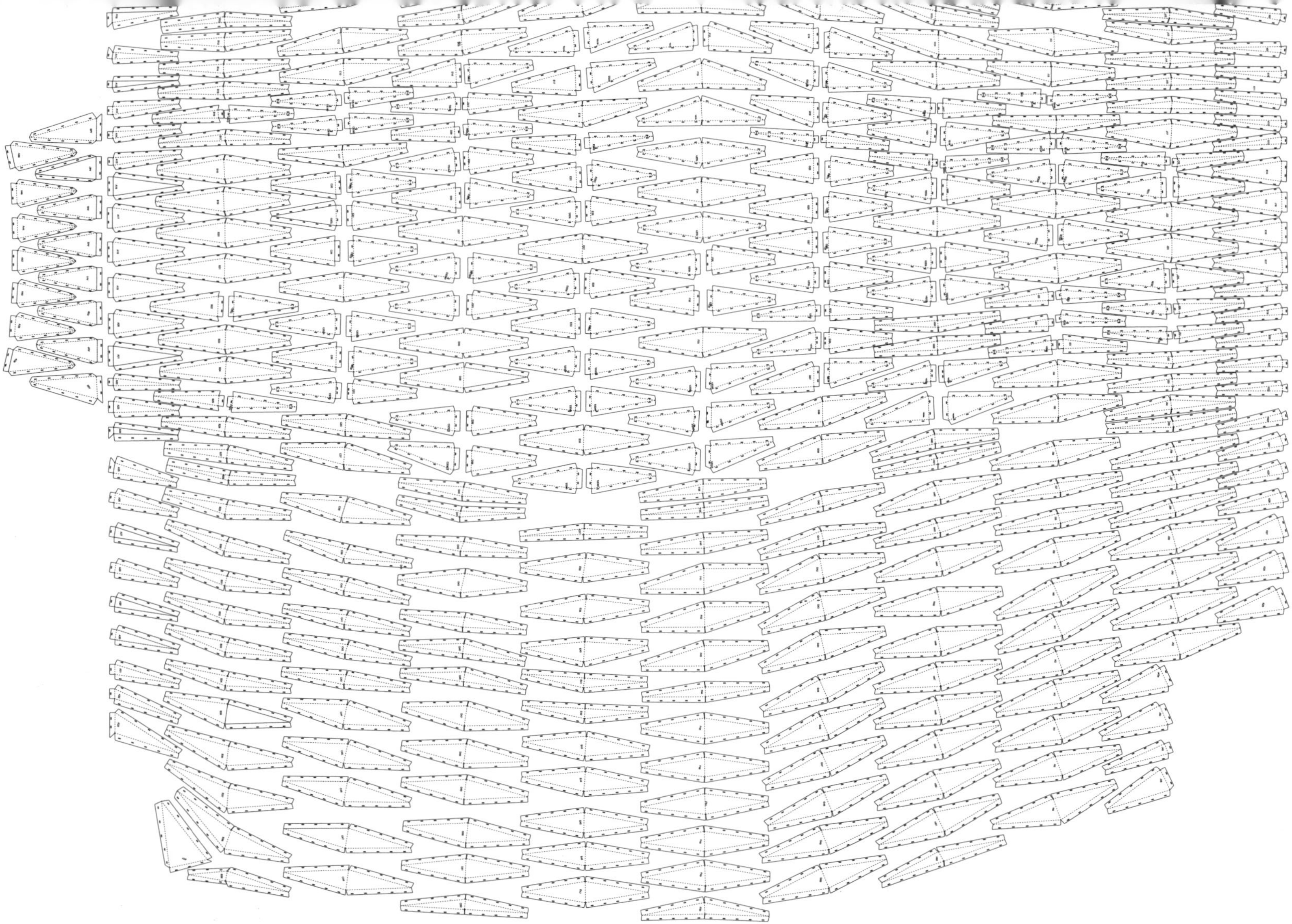

As a space for viewing, the Puppet Theater takes advantage of the unique conditions of the site. During a performance, the raked seating focuses attention on the stage. At other times, the orientation of the theater focuses a view outward toward the adjacent environment; a single tree is framed by the theater opening, creating a sense of spatial enclosure. The elongated diamond panels enclosing the theater serve to heighten this aspect of viewing as it creates perspectival distortions of the viewing space. Also, during the day, the surrounding environment is reflected into the theater by the gloss of the polycarbonate panels. In the evening, the relationship reverses as the theater becomes a glowing moss-covered lantern projecting outward onto the environment.

Ultimately, the parameters of site, fabrication, and structure had to fit within the constraints of the program: a puppet theater. Each parameter networked in concert with the others, simultaneously experimented, to arrive at the ultimate design.

PS1 Competition

This project was proposed for the 2007 P.S.1/MoMA Young
Architects Program Competition. The program called for a temporary summertime installation that also serves as the site for the
popular music and event series, Warm-Up. As a temporary home
for a seasonal event, the design took a typological look at traditional
nomadic Bedouin tent structures; the typological tent was adapted
for P.S.1 through the use of new materials and fabrication processes
that consider, as their constraints, the limitations of the site and
program. The main constraint of the project was budgetary:
the entire design and construction process was limited by a budget
of $60,000. To minimize the construction cost, the entire installa-
tion was prefabricated as a series of inflatable cells. Rather than rely
on a labor-intensive construction process, the design relied instead
on a deployment process that could inflate the entire canopy in
under one hour.

The material used is a technologically advanced 3D woven aluminized fabric, developed for aerospace and military applications, balancing unusual strength and durability with exceptional lightness. The canopy consists of a series of four hyperbolic paraboloids, each created from a series of inflatable cells. The hyperbolic paraboloid shape maximizes the structural capacity of canopy while minimizing the amount of material used. As a result, minimal energy would be needed to inflate and maintain pressure in the cells of the structure.

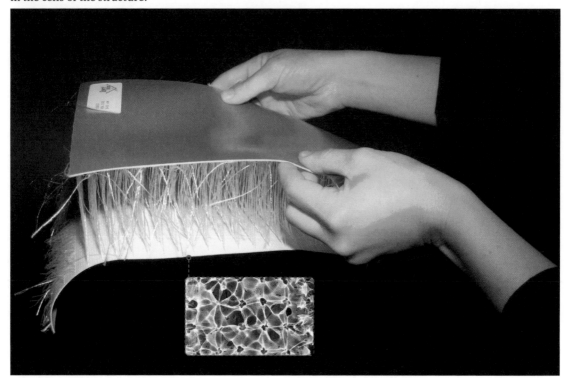

Within the parametric environment, the curvilinear surface of the canopy was disaggregated into a series of cellular sections. Each section of the larger canopy consists of a set of smaller hyperbolic paraboloid cells, optimized for structural support. The size and spacing of the cells were then evaluated in the digital environment to optimize material use, structure, views, and ventilation.

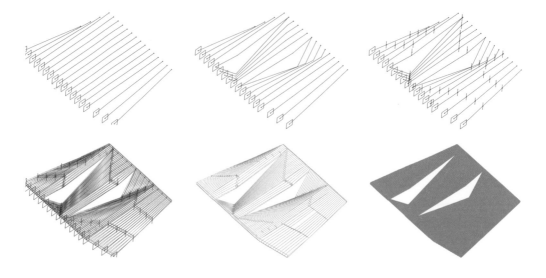

The gaps between cells create vents for the movement of air though the space underneath. The 3D material also has unique insulation and reflective properties, which create differences in temperature and pressure between the area under the canopy and the external environment. As a result, the canopy generates its own consistent breeze, promoting passive cooling while also maintaining a subtle shift and sway in the canopy cells themselves. This sway, coupled with the gloss of the material, dynamically reflects the activity occurring below.

At night, the cooler temperature causes a slight drop in the structure's air pressure, exaggerating the sway and movement of the canopy. When lit from below, the slackened canopy refracts light back into the covered space, casting a crystalline diffusion of light. Whereas the structure acts more as a protective tent in the daytime, reflecting sunlight away; at night, the relationship reverses, acting as a shimmering cave containing the glow of the light within.

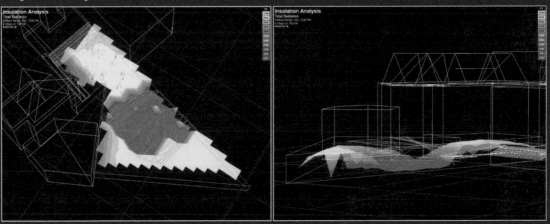

Insolation analysis

Within the courtyard, the plan of the canopy divides the larger space into discrete outdoor rooms, each connected by the covered structure. The canopy itself, in turn, is fractured into distinct spaces through the cellular arrangement of the four hyperbolic paraboloids. Although the canopy divides the larger courtyard into discrete spaces, it also creates visual connections through the gaps between cells of the canopy. While the canopy systematically divides space at multiple scales, the ground plane is contrasted by a system of growth, spreading throughout. A system of moveable seats allows a flexible, scalable, and customizable arrangement of seating throughout the courtyard. As single units, the seats can be used independently, stacked to create seating of varied height, or flipped over for use as a planter. Arranged together, the seats and planters create scalable arrangements of communal seating. In the largest arrangements, the system forms a varied landscape of seating.

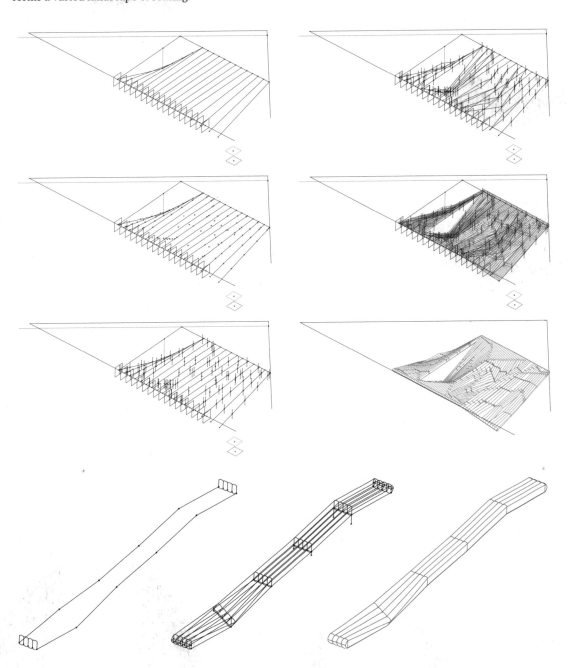

As a temporary structure, it was important for the design to take into account the lifecycle of the structure: after the Warm-Up series ends, all of the canopy material was to be recycled for use in disaster-relief structures. The seating units would be made available for sale as outdoor garden furniture, extending their life beyond the end of the Warm-Up series as well.

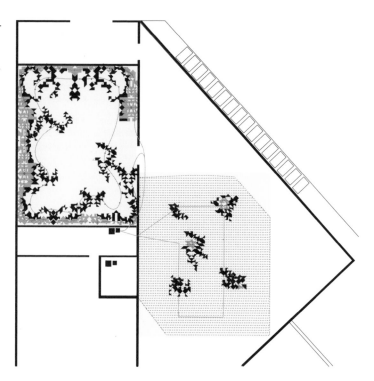

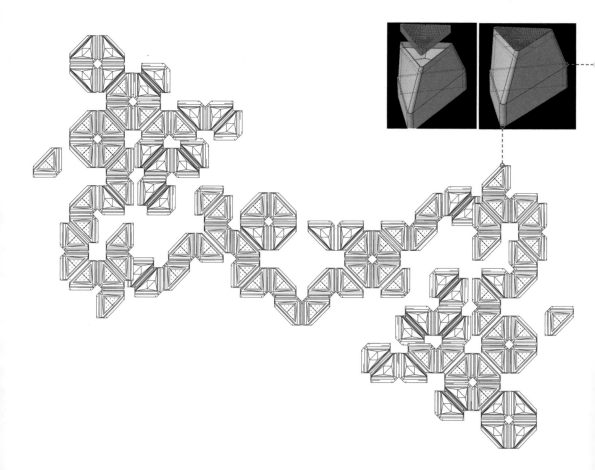

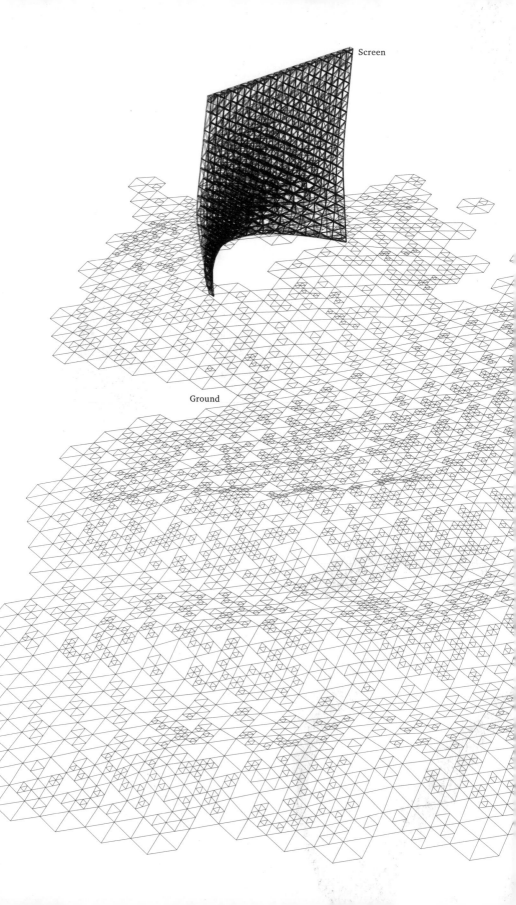

Screen

Ground

Ballroom drive-in

The Ballroom Marfa/MoMA drive-in theater is anything but typical. The theater does not only serve as a site for cinema, but also a multi-use site for theater, music, art and recreation. These programs, in turn, would exist within the unique context of the spectacular Marfa landscape. While the drive-in theater has a nostalgic presence in popular culture, the unique challenges of program and site in this project gives this historic typology a contemporary presence.

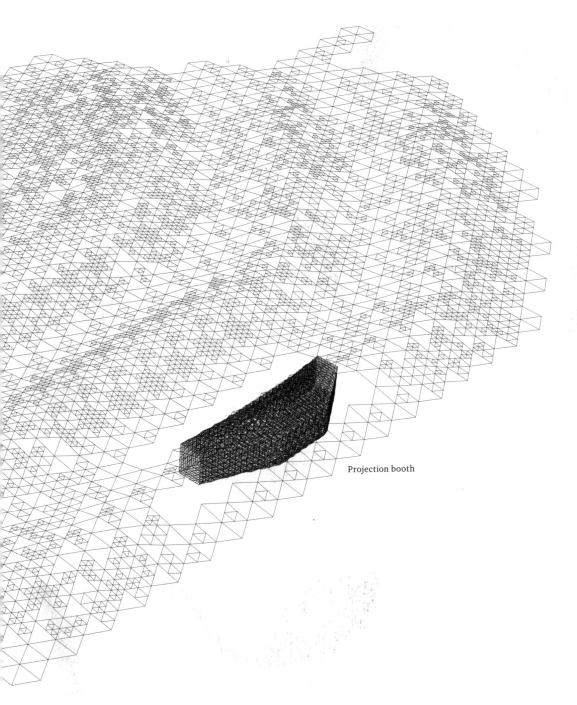

Projection booth

Screen The drive-In consists of three components: the screen, the landscape, and the projection booth. The design of the screen begins with the familiar typological form of the American drive-In. The typical Drive-In comprises a discrete screen backed by a separate structural system; at Marfa, both systems merge. The flat projection surface transitions into a curve as it meets the ground, creating a single unified free-standing structure: the space created by the curvature serves as a bandshell for music and theater performances. In this sense, the design of the screen is performative in both senses of the word: performing structurally as well as serving as a site for artistic performance. The curved form and multi-purpose program creates challenges for fabrication, acoustics, and structure. Working within the framework of Rhino scripting and Catia modeling, it is possible for the simultaneous experimentation, manipulation, and analysis of these competing systems in concert with one another. The curving surface of the screen was first divided in the parametric environment by a set of control points. As the points were incrementally manipulated, it was possible to evaluate the implications on structure, fabrication, acoustics and economics.

The result is a panelization that focuses on the permutation of a single hexagon (or six equilateral triangles), which in turn, facilitates the curvature of the screen. The hexagons are defined by a system of folded plates, which not only create structural rigidity, but also serve as an acoustic coffer for the bandshell. Moreover, the hexagonal panelization permits the curved form of the screen to be pre-fabricated from a system of flat hexagonal components. Only through the computation parametric environment can permit this simultaneous resolution of fabrication, performance, and structure with the constraints of form and program.

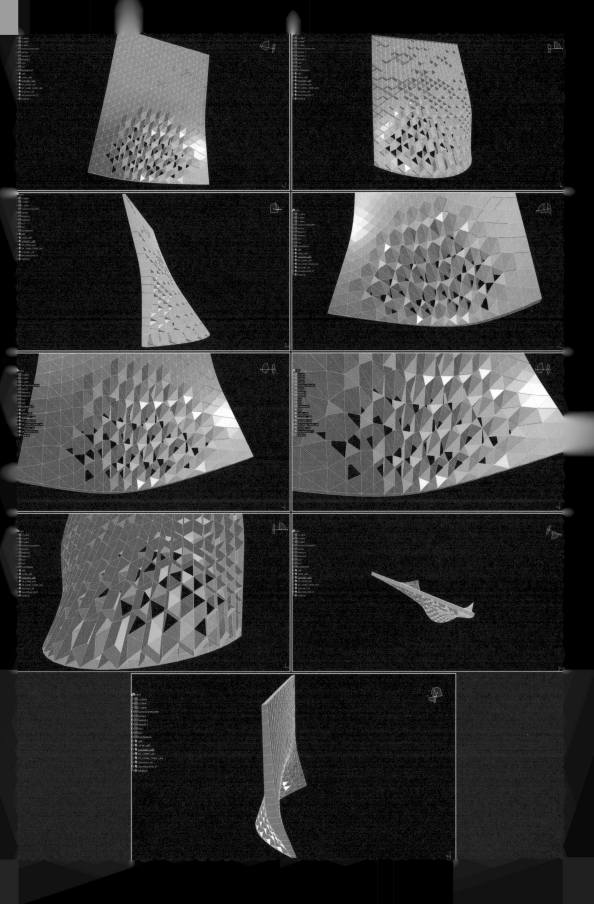

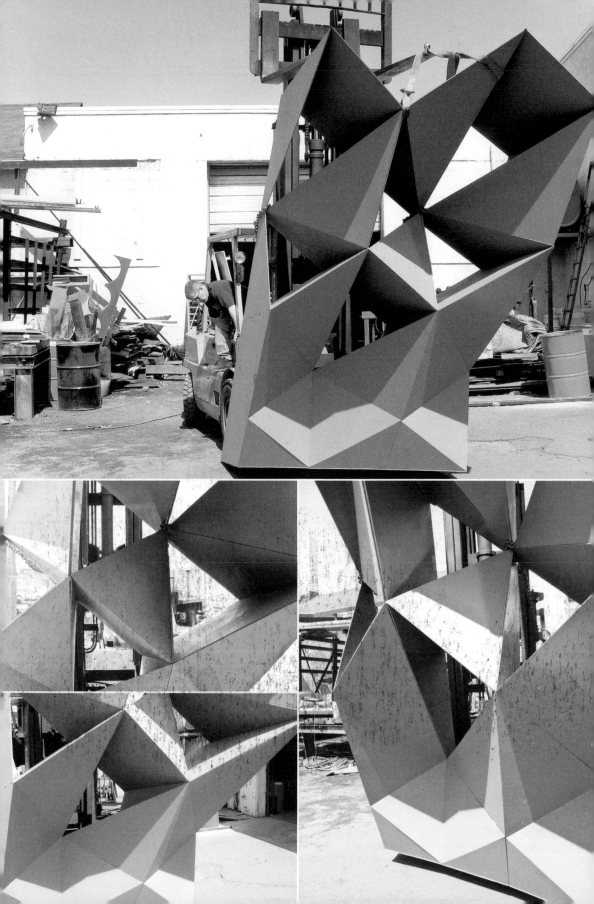

Projection booth

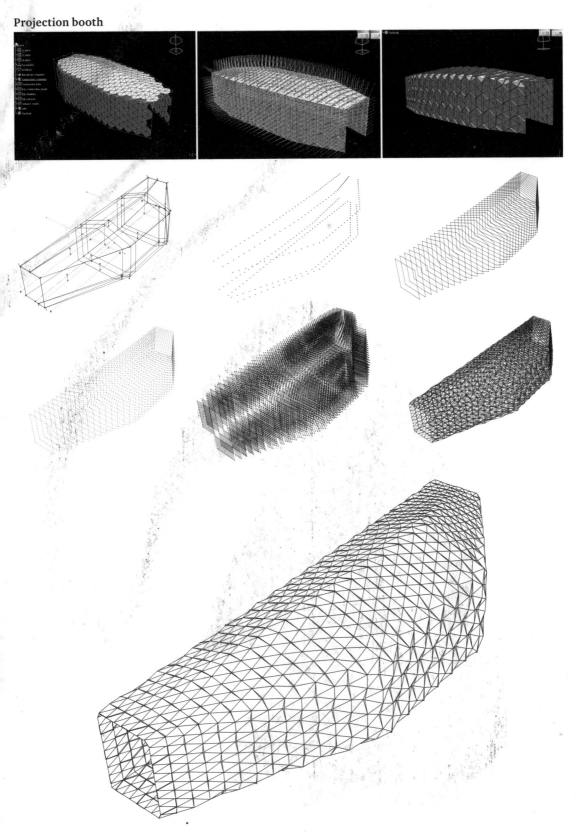

Ground The panelization and form of the screen also serves to create a unique relationship to the landscape around it. The ground is formed into a series of berms and mounds that are angled to optimize viewing of the screen, for both parked cars as well as pedestrians. The landscape orients each viewer into a direct relationship with the panelized screen, a relationship that is both intense and individualized. The manipulation and orientation of the ground ties together the screen, landscape, and projection booth; a concert of enclosure and spatial definition in an otherwise wide open desert.

Although a site for intensive viewing, when not in use for a specific event or performance, this space is open enough to take the form of a park, functioning in the round for recreational use and engaged with the vast Marfa landscape. The result of this dialectic of use is a tension between the boundless expanse of the desert plain and the bounded intimacy of the individual drive-in experience: a constant expansion and contraction of space at a scale that doesn't seem to exist anywhere else.

At the Marfa Drive-In, there is a merging of a multiplicity of use with boundaries of site, structure, fabrication of form. The result is a system of complexity that fosters interrelationships between different constituencies of the project. The goal is to promote the proliferation of individual narratives of meaning and use, ultimately nurturing explorations of the connections between cinema, theater, music and art to the landscape, as well as to each other.

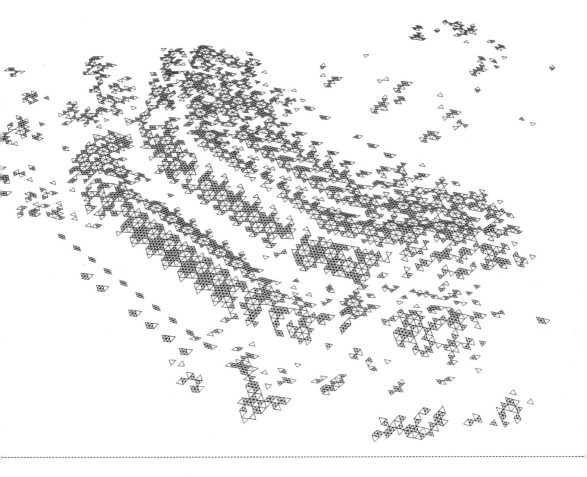

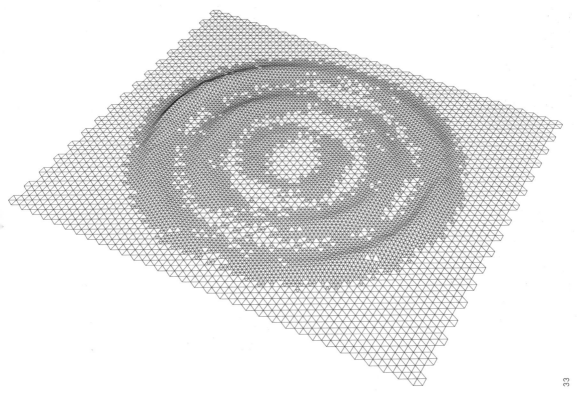

AGU
Advanced Geometry Unit at Arup

was founded by Cecil Balmond in 2000 as ARUP's think tank dedicated to researching complex structural geometry in support of new architectural visions and solutions. AGU has collaborated with many architects, scientists and engineers and realized a variety of remarkable buildings like the Serpentine Pavillions with Toyo Ito, Daniel Libeskind or Alvaro Siza, Centre Pompidou, Metz with Shigeru Ban, and the CCTV New Headquaters, Beijing with OMA. **www.arup.com**

"The dynamics of line and surface define the templates that create architecture and organisations. In the making of form it is not only shape that counts but the rules and interior logic by which such contours are derived. Probing these regimes is the research, understanding the results and putting them into practice is the work, and the AGU is the mix of architects, engineers and scientists that create designs, beyond mere style and fashion, to offer interest and beauty." –Cecil Balmond

The Advanced Geometry Unit at Arup is a multidisciplinary group of architects, engineers and scientists working together on the making of buildings, structures and environments. We came together in 2000 as a small group of people that shared common interests in the definition of a new practice. Architecture is either derivative of past models or pursuing sensation through exaggeration, usually engaged in the trivial mimicking of software-lofted surfaces: we wanted to build from first principles and our own prescriptions of forms based on interior dynamics that grow their own logic.

The approach is to accept as irreducible the notion of complexity; a holistic view, one that is different from the traditional methods of drawing sections and plans and then extruding or patching them to make buildings. For the AGU a form is not only a building but can be viewed as master plan, structure or sculpture—any organisation that interrogates space in new ways. We carry out our own designs and are also in a commitment to collaborate with other architects and designers. The AGU is an investigation into a new aesthetic.

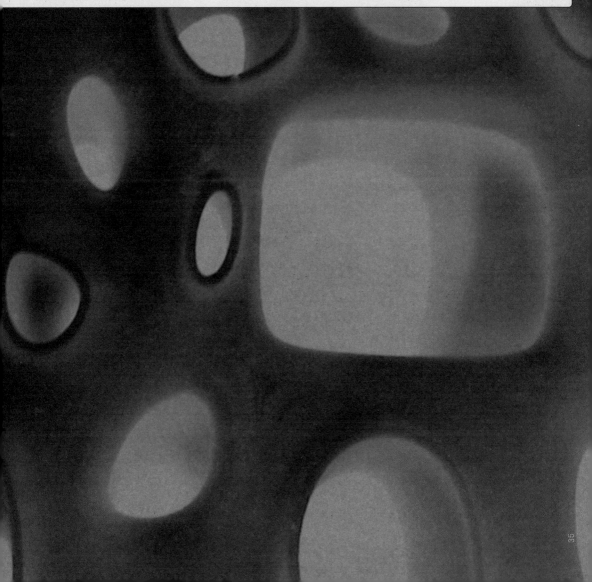

Geometric
Algorithm
Serpentine Gallery
Pavilion 2002
Toyo Ito & Associates, Architects
Cecil Balmond (Arup)

The Serpentine Gallery Pavilion 2002 designed with Toyo Ito, was an opportunity
to experiment with new geometric algorithms to structure and organise space.
Toyo Ito opened the dialogue with a sketch of a box with a series of random intersect-
ing lines on the roof and vertical columns. Our challenge became that of finding a rule,
an algorithm that would generate that chaos with its intricate beauties, but with
an underlying order that would allow the realisation of the pavilion in fourteen weeks.
The project started as a search of the key to creating complexity and richness pattern,
but with a simple rule that rationalised its geometry, structure and construction. In
the end we discovered the emergence of a completely new and unexpected aesthetic.

We set off on our research by taking the square plan of the pavilion and subdividing it with a rather arbitrary geometric rule. Our approach is very often to start from an arbitrary point and critically examine the multiple outcomes that yield from modifying the starting rule.

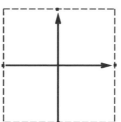

A Cartesian approach to the subdivision of the square would have led us to draw straight equidistant lines from one side to the opposite side in the two directions parallel to the sides of the square.

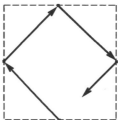

First, we considered that connecting two adjacent sides would generate shorter lines and subvert the Cartesian grid; This was enough to proceed! Secondly, we decided which points of the two adjacent lines to connect.

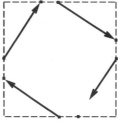

We considered that connecting half of each side to half of the next or one third of each side to the next would create squares completely inscribed within the first. We decided to avoid this by con-necting the half point of each side to the third point of the next: 1/2 to 1/3.

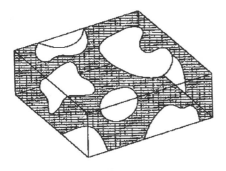

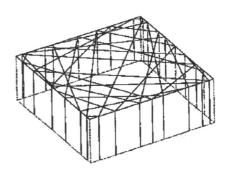

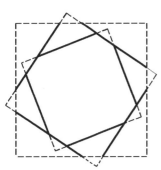

This construction yields a truncated, partially inscribed square within the first, the extension of its sides generating a square 0.xx the size of the parent.

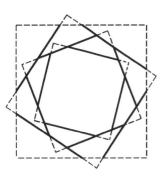

At this point our approach was to repeat the same geometric subdivision rule to the second square and then again to the third with a recursive process.

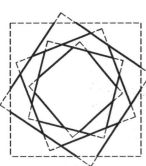

The 1/2 to 1/3 rule was combined with a 1/3 to 1/2 algorithm, generating similar angles between the lines, but different proportions between parent and child (0.xx).

The subdivision algorithm is repeated seven times producing a spiral of truncated squares. At this point all the lines are extended forming an infinite pattern that is folded from the roof to the wall of the box.

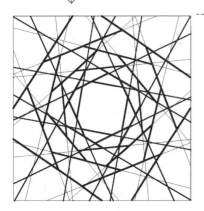

Structural hierarchies

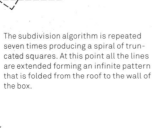

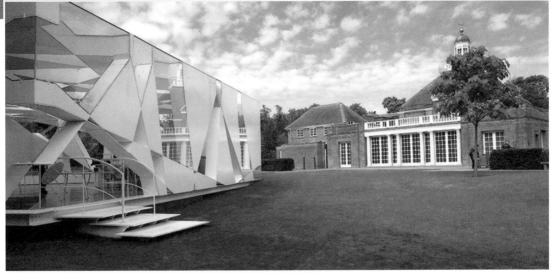

To generate structure the geometric pattern of lines is extruded 550 mm perpendicularly to its surface, thus roof lines become vertical bars acting as beams and wall lines become diagonal lines of a braced wall plane.
The connecting piece between wall and roof is the simplest vertical square plate perpendicular to the edge of the roof.

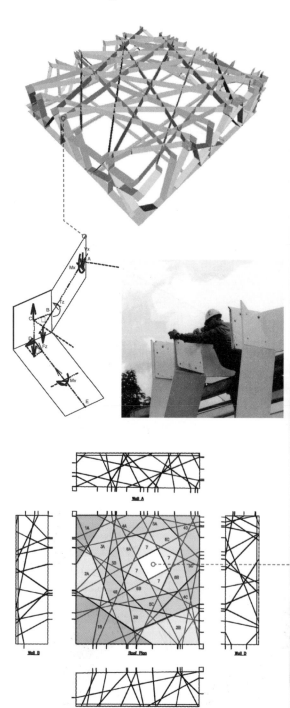

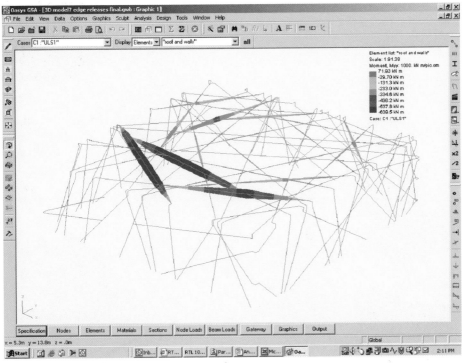

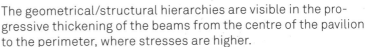

The structure of the pavilion inherits many of the hierarchies of its underlying geometry in that the primary spiral of squares becomes a primary ziggurat of beams, where each level of the ziggurat supports the inner ones and the secondary extensions of the core spiral becomes a series of secondary structural restraining members which avoids buckling of the primary beams.

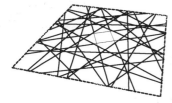

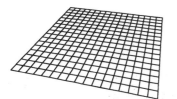

The geometrical/structural hierarchies are visible in the progressive thickening of the beams from the centre of the pavilion to the perimeter, where stresses are higher.

So the geometric rigors of the pavilion's generating algorithm offer structural hierarchies and efficiencies, but they also offer the opportunity of discretising the structure into a series of subcomponents more easily manageable from a transportation and erection point of view.

The structure is therefore conceived as a series of discrete panels reciprocally supporting and stabilizing one another in an interlocked spiralling composition. Each panel is invariably composed of a primary beam and a series of prewelded bracing members. Each connection between a primary beam and the next is the same geometrically, making fabrication and construction much simpler.

Reciprocity hierarchy and discreteness order and proportion

Rigors and complexity Complexity is achieved by recursive repetition of a simple rule from which stems the structure's geometry and detail. Within this complexity modularity and repetition are preserved and hierarchies order and govern processes of fabrication and construction.

Complexity is latent order not chaos. It keeps the eye in constant search for that hidden rule that moves and is lost within the spiralling patterns of lines that surround you.

And finally complexity generates pattern and ornament, tectonic in its nature and therefore indiscernible from the structure. The chequer-board pattern of solid and transparent cladding is a simple binary representation of the minimal but complex pattern derived by the 1/2 to 1/3 rule.

Reciprocity, Hierarchy and Discreteness
Serpentine Gallery Pavilion 2005

Alvaro Siza and Eduardo Souto de Moura
Cecil Balmond (Arup)

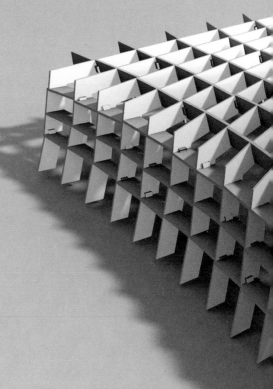

How to build a roof? Precedent leads to expectations of bold gestures, hierarchies of span, and dominating elements leaping over enclosed space. How can this be reversed? What if elements are equal and evenly distributed? What if they are each too short to achieve the span? What if they can only work in collaboration, relying on mutual support to create a spanning system?

Traditional timber construction methods evolved through their connection logic. The structural languages of the Japanese temple and English half-timbered house derive from their details: relationships between element and joint, continuity and splice defined their characters. Contemporary frames lose these idiosyncratic qualities; generic details reduce the logic to post and beam, primaries and secondaries – a mechanical array of elements between nodes.

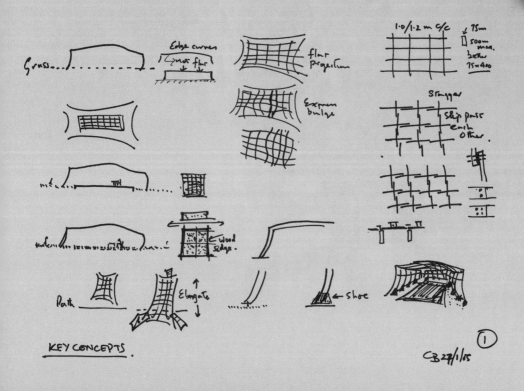

KEY CONCEPTS.

CB 27/1/05

With this pavilion, the starting point was the grid. The grid provides the armature for sculpting space and controlling the structure. Siza saw timber as the material and a grid as its framing vessel; Cecil Balmond saw the grid as a "template for action," a mechanism to be deformed, tuned through Siza's spatial sensitivity, to the context of the site. AGU took the grid, the intent, and explored the potential. How to allow the grid to deform but maintain a pattern? To be free-from but not amorphous? To articulate its geometry, but with subtlety? The starting point, the default grid structure, is the grillage; the word itself suggests structure trapped. Pragmatic concerns played a part: demountability favours man-handle-able components. Simple connections speed the assembly. An interlocking structure self-stabilises during erection. A simple set of rules defines each component. All elements are the same depth; mortice and tenon dimensions are fixed; the bottom edge is straight; the top edge kinked; and so on. By mathematically relating each of these rules to the surrounding nodes of the grid, the standard component (and hence all components) can be described. Coding these vector relationships into a script, the volumetric geometry of every component (427 in total, all different) could be produced automatically from an input geometry—the nodal definition of the underlying grid. Each component geometry was directly sent to the five-axis CNC router, making drawings redundant.

The reciprocal grid provided the solution. Each discrete element is two grid-bays long. It is supported by locking its ends into neighbouring elements, and at the same time supports its neighbours.

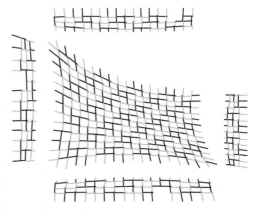

There is no clear load-path and no structural hierarchy: forces loop, pinwheel-style, through the structure until perimeter support is reached. The structural diagram, of discrete elements with pin-ended connections, allows simple mortice and tenon connections (bending forces do not need to be transferred).

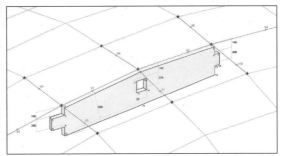

The ends of two elements meet, in a rectangular hole at mid-point of a third.

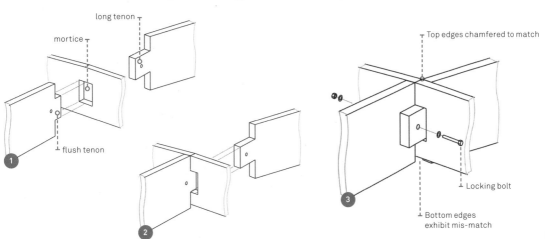

The alternate offset of the elements (a logical consequence of the double mortice and tenon) creates shuffles and slips in the grid. The static grillage becomes a dynamic network, the pieces tumbling in their eccentric positions—each displaced from the underlying grid. The subtleties of the generative rules dictate the slips. As the elements accommodate greater deformations of the grid, the deliberate mismatches are amplified. These slips have an ornamental quality; an intentional consequence of the assembly logic, permitted for the purpose of expressing this logic (the mismatches could have been eliminated by a tweak to the script), they create a pattern superimposed on the structure itself.

This ornamentation has been designed without direct architectural authorship. Responsibility has been devolved. Determined solely by the automated definition process, no condition is individually designed. The effect is not random or accidental, but it is locally uncontrolled —determined only by the global decisions on the rules that dictate the bounds and format of the slips. The formal result has a biomorphic quality (Alvaro Siza conceived the pavilion as a "crouching animal"), reflecting how nature arranges discrete components in larger systems.

The overall result risks being one of contradiction—a clash of traditional detail and high technology—but the result instead is more like a contemporary vernacular. The key is in the connection detail, precisely fabricated yet crudely assembled, its medieval simplicity is what unlocks the life of the whole grid.

Alishan Tourist Routes

Reiser + Umemoto, Taiwan 2003

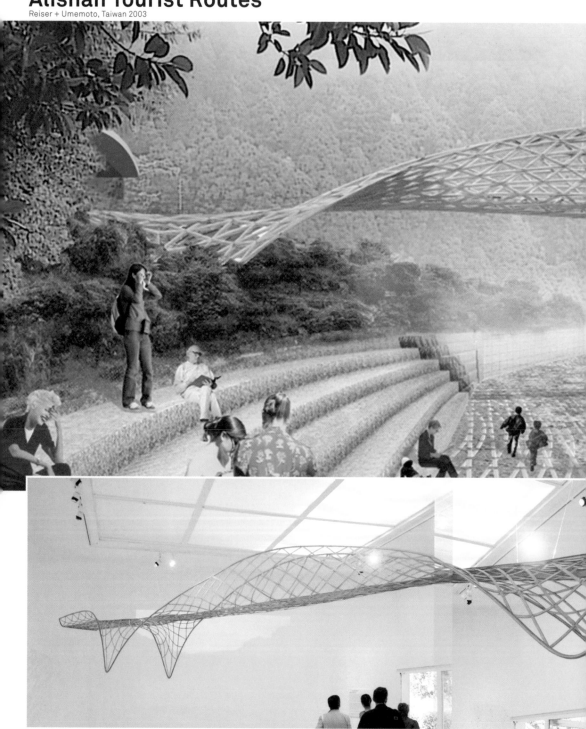

Reiser + Umemoto's winning competition entry for the Alishan tourist routes project consists of two railway stations, a visitor- and community centre and the Fenquihu Bridge, iconic entry of the development. The local government was looking for an innovative architectural design to stimulate local tourism in a remote location in the Alishan Mountains nearby Taipei.

The Venice Architecture Biennale model
The lattice grid structure of the Fenquihu Bridge was first presented as a 1:10 scale physical model at the 2004 Venice Architecture Biennale. The intention of the 8 metre-long timber model is to represent the architectural idea of a woven basket in its purest sense.

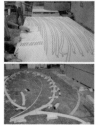

The lattice was composed of 120 timber strips, milled out of 5 mm plywood sheets. The unrolling of each strip, hand-sculpted by the architect, from the design surface and marking its intersection points created the flattened geometry. With the help of a series of jigs, the strips were then bent and joined into a doubly-curved lace. The circular edge members were built up in a similar way by composing a square 3D curved member from flattened strips and then shaped manually into a circular geometry.

The final model represents the spatial intent of the bridge, but because of its flexible nature the lace was not able to demonstrate a structural behaviour. While the longitudinal edges define the primary structural elements—two leaning arches in the centre, back span beams on one side and cantilevers on the other—these needed to be restrained by the internal grillage to enable the surface to keep its shape. Whilst the flexibility of flat timber strips was advantageous to build the diagonals of the physical model, the real structure of these elements will require far more stiffness.

Timber ribs The real-scale analysis of the competition geometry showed that the meshing of the members was too ambitious for a timber structure for various reasons. The diagonal set out generated a long path to travel for the dominating bending forces. Furthermore, timber structures are generally governed by their connections which in this case had to transfer moments and therefore made the firstly stated even worse.

Hence a more hierarchical system composed of bending stiff transversal ribs and stabilizing diagonals was developed. Also, the shape of the surface needed to be structurally rationalized further. A structurally more rigorous surface was defined by using the two longitudinal edges of the surface as guiding rails for arc-shaped transversal ribs. The resulting design worked very well in structural terms but also showed the applied engineering principles in an eminent way. The design team decided to explore more options focusing on a more unpredictable expression of structure and space.

Single-layered tapered

When determining the intrinsic design elements of the bridge, it came down to the shape of the surface and its diagonal meshing. The diagonals were then reduced to 180 mm deep and wide H-sections to minimally represent the grillage. The doubly-curved nature of the surface is emphasized by bending and twisting the sections along their path. The tapering of the members at the cantilevered end of the viewing platform allows the grillage to resist against the higher moments in this area. Large openings in the web of these tapered beams provide visual lightness. A geometric rigger was established and articulated in a Visual Basic script to investigate different meshing options in an efficient way. A series of longitudinal lines on the design surface—the isopharms of a NURBS—are used as the generating skeleton of the diagrid. By defining the number of subdivisions for these lines an array of intersection points is generated which is connected to the final grid. Parallel to the generating process of the geometry the script produces the input data for the structural model. Every option tested is immediately ready for analysis after the geometry is processed. Structure and form merged at a stage where neither the formal shape nor pragmatic engineering principles dominated the design. The design process settled in-between the two attractors of form and force creating a new tectonic form.

Double-layered steel

The client welcomed shifting the structural material from timber to steel as he raised concerns regarding the life span of a timber structure. The edge members consist of doubly-curved, 300 mm-diameter tubular sections. The diagonal grillage is formed by a double-layered steel plate structure, picking up the weaving concept of the competition scheme. Two layers of 250 mm-wide steel flats, spaced at 300 mm, wrap around the design surface and are connected at their intersections. This provides sufficient bending stiffness of the diagonal elements. To achieve the additional structural depth required at the cantilevering end, the two layers separate to form a diamond-shaped truss. The whole geometry was represented through a customised computer script, which also enabled an automated unfold of the steel plate strips. The chosen system represents both the architectural and structural intentions of at project. The desired shape of the surface could be realized by a bending system that was able to adjust its structural depth to form the cantilever. A disadvantage was that the integrated centre truss divided the viewing platform into two parts. Furthermore, the twin plate system behaves as a Vierendeel truss, which transfers its shear forces mainly through weak axis bending of the two chords. This resulted in the plates being wider and thicker than desired, which created visual and physical heaviness.

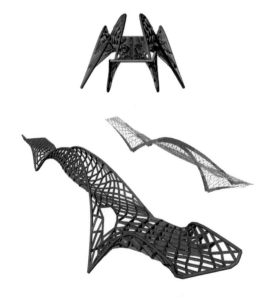

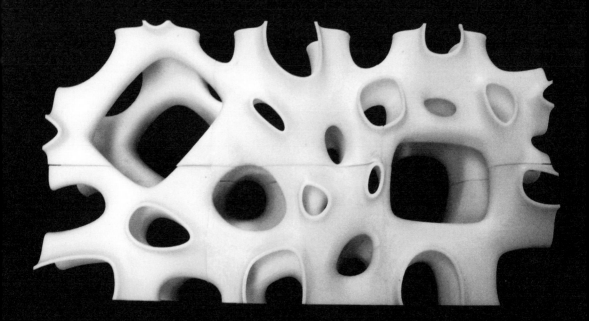

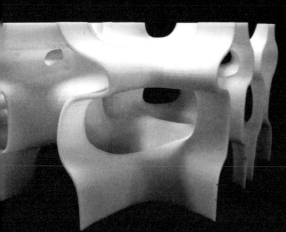

Taichung
Metropolitan
Opera House

Toyo Ito & Associates, Architects
Taiwan, estimated completion 2009

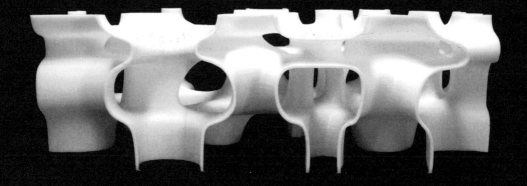

Toyo Ito's winning competition proposal for the Taichung Metropolitan Opera House comprises exciting challenges to the complexity of geometry and structural analysis. To realize the ambitious design the AGU developed a series of specific geometry and structural model generating tools.

The emerging grid The intention was to create a space without orientation. A rectangular box defines a perimeter border in which a continuous surface is placed. This surface divides the space into cavities which can form an exterior or interior part of the building.

The smoothness of the surface is favoured not only for aesthetic reasons, but as an essential condition to obtain an efficient structural system. The shell-type structure doesn't distinguish between wall and slab as their transitions are continuously accrued.

By using a smoothing subdivision algorithm like Catmull-Clark, the surface is controlled by an array of polygonal quad facets that provide the starting geometry for the process. Each facet is subdivided into a new set of vertices and then averaged between their adjacent neighbours. The crude starting grid densifies and transforms—it is emerging.

Geometry smoothing process The prototype of the algorithm was initially developed for the concrete shell roof of the Arnhem Central Station, designed by UNStudio. Composing a complex surface from multiple single NURBS patches while preserving a smooth curvature transition along the seams is still a challenge for current CAD software.

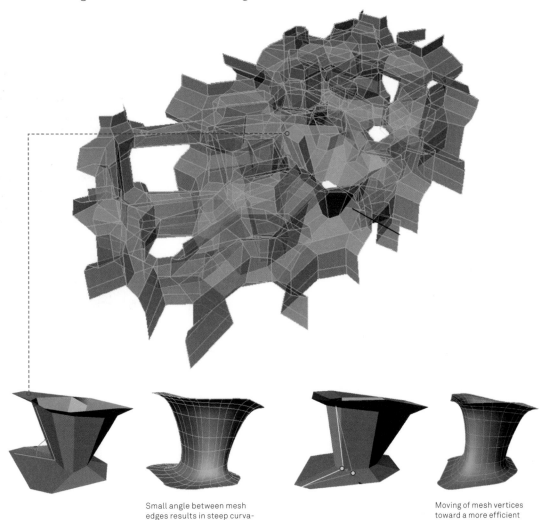

Small angle between mesh edges results in steep curvature of the smooth surface.

Moving of mesh vertices toward a more efficient structural set out.

The adopted smoothing algorithm is able to describe an infinite surface as a single object. Smooth transitions are ensured by the process and generated by the interpolation of the neighbouring vertices. To gain full control over the process and the ability to extract specific data during the execution, the algorithm was programmed from scratch by using Rhinoceros as visualisation engine. Specific requirements suggested by the project's geometry were added to the process. All vertices coinciding with the subscribing box are constrained on this perimeter and are only allowed to perform a 2D smoothing. After the smoothing is performed and a new set of geometry objects is created, the topology and connectivity of the elements is detected and attached as user data to the drawing objects.

Structural model generation The software used to analyse the structure requires only the edge curves of a doubly-curved surface to execute an inbuilt meshing algorithm that approximates the area with a so-called Coons patch. A wire frame of edge curves and their corner points is sufficient to describe the whole structure. The algorithm browses through all geometry elements extracting their attached topology and connectivity data and writes a simple ASCI input file which can be executed instantly in the FE [Finite Element] package. Also loading patterns, support conditions and material data is already included in the processed model.

The minimum data set that needs to be communicated with the architect is reduced to the crude mesh information. The developed tools enable the creation of a structural model in an optimized process and an almost instant response to design changes. In reverse, structural optimized versions of the mesh geometry can be proposed and communicated back in the same way.

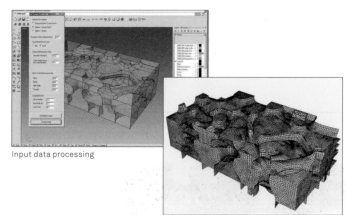

Input data processing

FE mesh

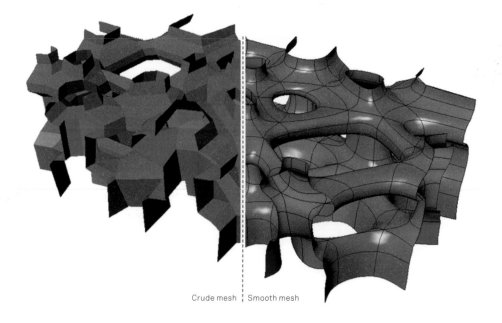

Crude mesh ¦ Smooth mesh

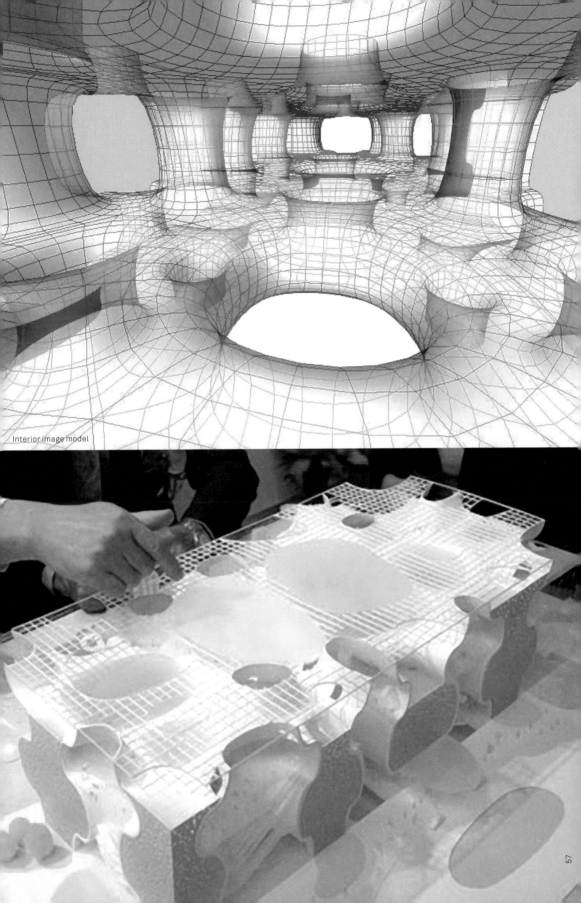

Interior image model

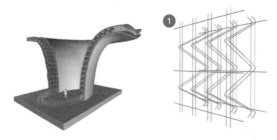

Catenoid structure At competition stage, a double-layered composite steel structure using sprayed concrete was proposed.
A grillage of curved steel beams defines the geometry. Expanded metal sheets attached to the beams are flexible enough to follow the curvature and act as the formwork for the spray-on concrete. This option wasn't developed further as sprayed concrete technology is relatively uncommon in Asia and only used for nonstructural purposes.

Keeping the steel structure combined with conventional shuttering didn't seem to be sensible as in addition to the complex steel structure an equivalently complex shuttering system—for example CNC-milled Styrofoam—would be required.

Therefore a concrete-only option was developed with internal void formers to reduce the self-weight. Instead of using mild profile steel a series of parallel Warren trusses made of reinforcement steel are defining the geometry. Each sub panel of the catenoids—defined by the crude mesh geometrt—is cut parallel at various spacing. The so received planar curves deliver the geometry of the two chords of the respective trusses.

Void formers are placed in between and additional structural reinforcement is attached on both sides. Three layers of expanded metal sheets provide the formwork for the in situ self-compacting concrete. Finally, a manually-rendered finish is applied on the rough surface. Only with the help of tools specifically developed for the project was it possible to preserve the challenging architectural concept. By incorporating geometry processing techniques from other disciplines and linking them to structural analysis the boundaries of complex forms in construction are pushed to new limits.

Spacestation Diary
Tristan Simmonds

Blind Light
Antony Gormley, Hayward Gallery, London 2006-2007

End of November 2006

Invitation from Antony Gormley to visit his studio to look at a proposal for a large piece for his forthcoming show *Blind light* at the Hayward Gallery in London. A foam model is presented, a fetal figure made from boxes of a number of different sizes based on a regular grid unit. The sculpture is to fill the 6 m height of the gallery and sit on the corner points of three boxes. Each box is to be made of steel plate with square perforations to give "windows," indicating the grid. The sculpture is particularly complex and, ideally, will be modeled directly on computer.

However, Antony's team does not have much digital modeling experience.

The Gormley Boxer program is written to enable Adam at Antony's studio to intuitively place touching boxes of a set number of sizes within a volume defined by a full body scan of Antony in a fetal position. Adam starts modeling the sculpture using the Boxer program and simultaneously makes models using foam boxes, so that we have identical digital and physical representations. Discussion of the fixing details with Dave Mason from fabricator Sheetfabs. Agree on unobtrusive bolted connection using oversized holes in one box face with tapped holes in the adjoining box face. Each connection will have a bolting direction. Adam completes both a 355-box digital and physical model. Start writing GormBox Rhino plugin in C++ to process output from Boxer program. Generate booleaned solid model of sculpture and produce a rapid prototype. Prototype takes three days to build.

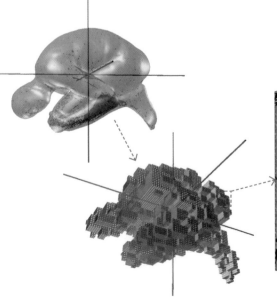

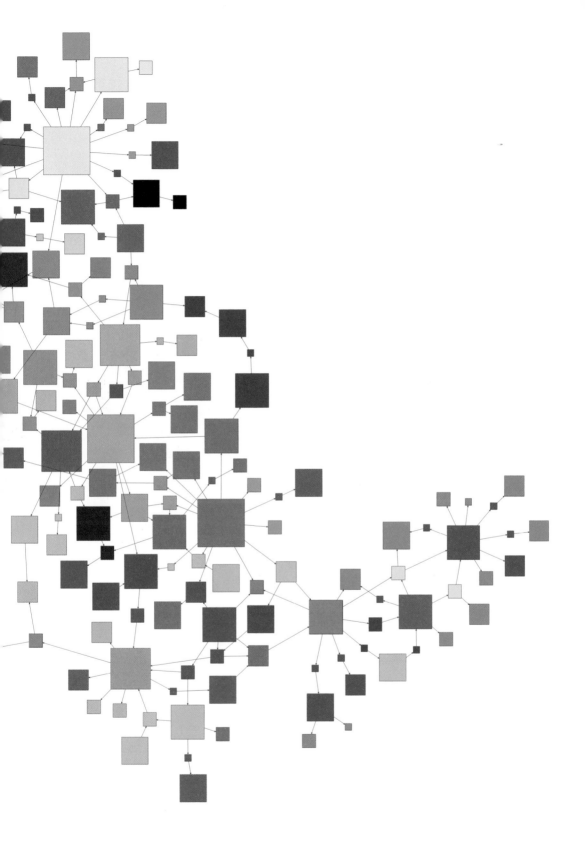

63

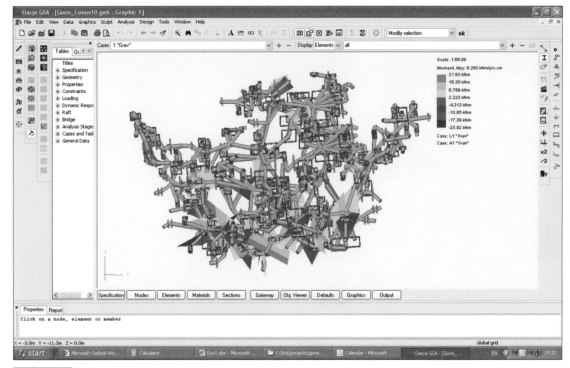

The GormBox plugin loads data from the Boxer program, processes it and builds a relational data structure of boxes, faces and connections. The boxes are automatically oriented so that Corner 0 is the lowest corner on the box in order to receive a drain hole. GormBox writes out a simplified representation for analysis of the connections in GSA structural analysis software and reloads the results to automatically design the size and arrangements of bolts for each of the 444 connections. GormBox writes out an 800,000-element detailed analysis model to examine deflection, face buckling and corner crushing of the entire sculpture. It takes a long time to analyse. A number of boxes are inserted and positions tweaked using the Boxer to help reduce stresses and deflections. GormBox "records" the reverse construction sequence carried out by removing boxes manually in Rhino and automatically sets the bolt direction for each connection. As a test the unwrapped patterns of the seven boxes that make up the head are drawn up manually using information from the Rhino model and sent for laser cutting. Each face is engraved with box number, face number, adjacent face number, connection outline, adjoining box number, bolt hole positions and tap size where required. Create an interactive VR walkthrough to allow Antony to walk around the gallery and position sculptures within the space.

Sheetfabs fabricate the seven boxes and assemble the head in their workshop using a simple construction sequence of a list of box numbers. The assembly goes well and so the bolt hole tolerance is reduced along with the size of the drain hole in each box. The Rhino plugin is significantly extended to produce developed patterns with engraved annotation for every box automatically in a format suitable for laser cutting. All patterns are sent for laser cutting. More analysis is carried out to determine which boxes require 12mm plate or reinforcement. Patterns for five boxes to be made from 12 mm plate are sent for laser cutting. A set of tools is added to the Rhino plugin to allow navigation and grouping of the construction sequence. Parts of the construction sequence are analysed to determine minimal stable structure termed the "Bridge". Sheetfabs start fabricating boxes in order of construction sequence.

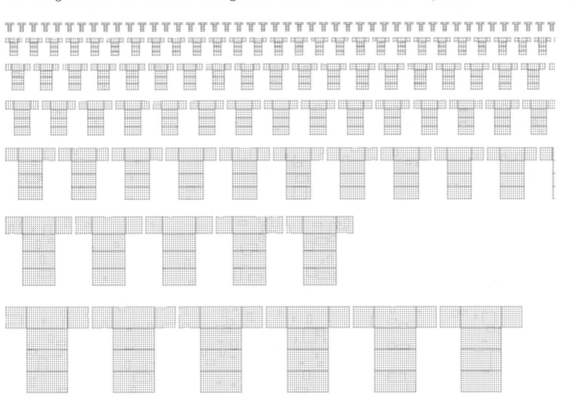

The first thirty boxes that make up the bridge are trial erected in Nottingham by a small team from Antony's studio and Sheetfabs. The outcome is positive with the decision that as much of the sculpture as possible is to be constructed on the horizontal before tipping it into its tilted resting position on three points.

> Further analysis of the construction sequence and de-propping modeling sequence.
> Surveyed Hayward Gallery for positioning of under-floor props.
> Determined temporary propping required for construction and loading on floor.
> Set out the support points and areas suitable for temporary propping on gallery floor.
> Submitted method statements and risk assessments to the Hayward Gallery.
> Gantries delivered to the Hayward Gallery.
> First batch of boxes delivered to the Hayward Gallery.
> Construction starts Monday 26 March.
> Construction is well ahead of schedule and de-propping is brought forward by a week.
> Friday 29 March, 60% complete, de-propping, lowering and rotating of sculpture onto its three support points. Tense but goes without a hitch.

The sculpture is
finished well
ahead of schedule.

May 2007
Wednesday 16 May, opening party.

Mutsuro Sasaki

is a professor at Hosei University, founded his structural engineering office in Tokyo in 1980. He is a major figure in Japanese architecture, collaborating with many architects in the realization of innovative buildings such as the Sendai Mediatheque with Toyo Ito or the Sapporo Dome with Hiroshi Hara. Sasaki develops new methodological approaches based on evolution and self-organization principles in response to new design developments in architecture.

Morphogenesis of Flux Structure: From the realization of free 3D forms by architects to evolving the most logical structure by computer calculation

1. Using the computer as a correction tool. How to adjust free, complex, amorphous, fluctuating organic forms to a buildable structure.

Sensitivity Analysis method:
A method for producing logical free curved surfaces closer to those drawn by architect.

Examples:
– National Grand Theatre competition in Beijing with Arata Isozaki
– Kitagata Community Centre with Arata Isozaki
– The Island City Central Park in Fukuoka with Toyo Ito
– The Crematorium in Kakamigahara with Toyo Ito

2. Using the computer to create a shape.

How to create unknown but logical structural form beyond our empirical knowledge?
Extended Evolutionary Structure Optimization (Extended ESO) method:
A method to generate the most effective 3D structural form (Flux Structure) from its dimension/load condition

Examples:
– Florence New Station competition with Arata Isozaki
– Qatar Education City Convention Centre with Arata Isozaki

In the international field of contemporary structural design, the theme has now become the creation of new three-dimensional architectural structures that possess free, complex, mutable, fluid and organic characteristics, thus expanding the architectural field. However, in order to achieve these in a truly rational way, traditional empirically-based structural design methods must be replaced with mathematically-based shape design methods that unify mechanics and aesthetics. The shape design techniques I employ are the Sensitivity Analysis method and the Extended Evolutionary Structure Optimization method. These involve generating rational structural shapes on a computer by using the principles of evolution and self-organization of living creatures from an engineering standpoint. I am currently experimenting with the application of these methods to the creation of new architectural structures. One example of their practical application is in free-curved surface structures, and another is in flux structures. The following pages offer a chance to understand the shapes and spaces of future architectural structures that use these shape design methods.

0.0 Preface

Turning point to think of the new structure method
Sendai Mediatheque project, Toyo Ito, 1995–2000

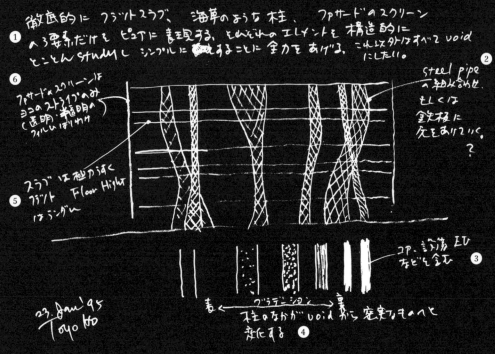

Sketch by Toyo Ito from the competition phase

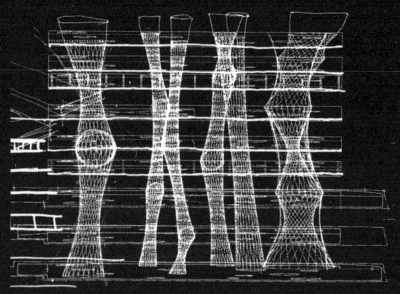

Sketch of structural elements by Mutsuro Sasaki

1 Complete flat slab, seaweed-like columns, screen façade, express only these three elements in the purest way, study each element structurally, and simplify them as much as possible, all the rest is left as a void • 2 Crossed steel pipe, or punch-holes on steel plate • 3 Include circulation cores or fitting • 4 front-gradation-back content of the columns varies from void to solid • 5 Thinnest slab, random floor height • 6 Screen façade has only horizontal strips (with transparent or translucent film)

This architectural proposal won a competition in 1995 and was completed in 2000. While I was struggling with Toyo Ito's initial sketch (opposite page) showing an amorphous image as if it were free of gravity, I proposed the idea of a minimal pure Domino steel structural system composed of 7 thin steel sandwich plates and 13 steel tubes. In the end I eventually managed to realize it after a lot of effort.

The experience in the Sendai Mediatheque was a big turning point that transformed my architectural and structural thinking, and I started looking for a new structural design beyond an empirical method to produce freer structural shapes.

1.0 Sensitivity Analysis method

Purpose of the research

- To create theoretically rational free curved surface by numerical analysis
- To comprehend and inspect the mechanical character of the created free curved surface

One existing technique for defining the shape of free-curved surfaces is the physical model experimental method used in the work of Antoni Gaudí, Heinz Isler and Frei Otto. Another is the method used in the competition for Beijing's National Grand Theatre, with Arata Isozaki (see next page), which involves a long period of trial-and-error in which the curved surface imagined by the architect is expressed using spline functions, followed by the structurally examined stress and deformation of the shell by FEM analysis, making local modifications to parts with structural problems. I wondered if a computer could be used for the application of mathematically based mechanical theory to generate structural shapes for the shape analysis of a real structural design.

Gaudí's suspended model with weights

Heinz Isler's Deitingen gas station, Swiss 1968

Naturally, as these are unseen shapes for free-curved shells, they would need to be given a strict engineering analysis based on their specific mechanical characteristics. I have been carrying out research on this topic at the university since the year 2000.

Sensitivity Analysis, which is an optimization method of shape analysis for the generation of free-curved shells. Form-resistant shell structures are ideally in a state of minimal stress and deformation. In other words, it could be said that minimal strain energy in the structure is the mechanically optimal condition. To put it the other way round, mechanically optimal shell structures are obtained by seeking the curved surface shape that generates minimum strain energy in the structure. The fundamental equation is given by differentiating the reference variable, strain energy by design parameter Z. For example, when a particular node is slightly altered, the effects on the strain energy of the entire structure C can be examined. The differential coefficient expressing the degree of change is, mechanically speaking, the Sensitivity Coefficient, and by seeking the Sensitivity Coefficient of all such nodes and checking the gradient of change in the strain energy, this can be optimized by revising the value of Z in the direction that will reduce the strain energy. The criteria for judging when convergence has occurred is a state in which there is no visible change in the strain energy after an evolutionary step.

When I joined the competition of the National Grand Theatre in Beijing with Arata Isozaki in 1998, it took many days of trial and error, but here it was all done in a very short time by a computer following a programmed algorithm. Incidentally, the problem is that we do not know where the non-linear solution will converge in relation to the initially established shape. It is necessary to establish an initial shape that is close to the desired shape, following which a relatively high-powered computer will get to something close to the desired shape in 10 or 15 minutes—evaluating how much a transformation at a node influences to the strain energy's transition in the whole structure.

National Grand Theatre, Beijing, competition with Arata Isozaki, 1998

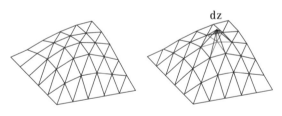

Formulation

Design Parameter: Shape (z Coordinates)
Evaluation Function: Strain Energy C

Sensitivity coefficient

Focussing on the transition of strain energy during transformation dz at node No. i in a structure composed by "n" elements.

$$C = \frac{1}{2}\{f\}^T\{u\}$$

$$[K]\{u\} = \{f\}$$

$$a_i = \frac{dC}{dz_i} = \frac{1}{2}\{u\}^T \frac{d(\Sigma_e[K_e^{(i)}])}{dz_i}\{u\}^T$$

{f} Nodal load vector
{u} Nodal displacement vector
[K] Element stiffness matrix
$\Sigma_e[K_e^{(i)}]$ Sum of element stiffness matrix related to node No. i

$$z_i' = z_i - a_i \Delta z$$

z_i' z coordinate after modification
z_i z coordinate before modification
$a_i \Delta z$ Parameter for adjusting modification amount

Modification of shape

ai > 0

in case of increases in the strain energy by the transformation at node "i"
→ Pull down its z coordinate

ai < 0

in case of decreases in the strain energy by the transformation at node "i"
→ Push up its z coordinate

1.1 Sensitivity Analysis method
Kitagata Community Centre
Arata Isozaki, 2002

Model of initial geometry derived by the
architect from the programme and other
project requirements.

Calculation in progress

After a few steps (10-15 minutes calculation), the
shape evolves to become rational and stabilized

Application to structural design

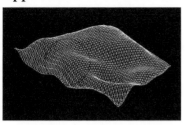

Step 1:
Initial shape
-Curved surface imaged by the architect
-Volumes required by the architectural function

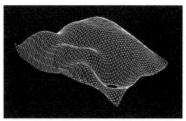

Step 20:
Final shape providing the rational shape that reflects the architect's intention (the part indicated by a red circle has evolved a great deal)

Final design: the result is a 15 cm-thick reinforced concrete shell with an amorphous shape like a piece of fabric, which covers the community centre as a roof.

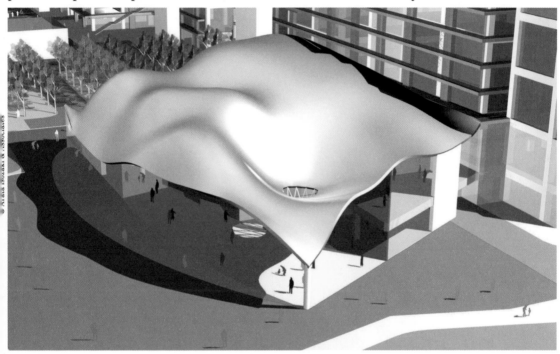

By Spring 2002 our research in my laboratory had managed to get to the stage of becoming a theoretical design method, and I urgently wanted to try using this shape analysis method on a real structure. The opportunity arose with Arata Isozaki's Kitagata Community Centre. The initial conditions of the building in terms of height and volume, together with its functional requirements decided by the architect, were established as the design parameters.

Then, using the shape analysis method explained above, the design variables were modified by a computer with a rigorous mechanical basis while we went on looking for an interesting shape. To determine the best shape, we altered the various design parameters several times. The designer was able to select the most interesting shape from among these. In this way, the roof became a 15 cm reinforced concrete shell with an amorphous shape like a piece of fabric.

With the Kitagata Community Centre as the first trial, we began to feel that this shape analysis method was adequate for use as a design tool.

This is a core facility for the park in a reclaimed island. Toyo Ito also wanted to employ free-curved surfaces using shape analysis; shown here is a free-curved surface shell designed in 2003 using another approach. The Island City Central Park in Gringrin, Fukuoka, comprises three continuous free-curved reinforced concrete shells with an overall length of 190 m, a maximum width of 50 m, and a thickness of 40 cm. An undulating helix in which the outer surface and the inner surface are reversed in two places, this is an extremely complex structural shape with an overall topological continuity between outside and inside. In this case, Toyo Ito had strong preferences for the shapes, so first we had a physical model of the desired shape produced, and then made slight modifications to this in the areas that were significantly at variance with the principles of shell structures. Taking this as the initial shape, we subjected it to the shape analysis operation I mentioned before.

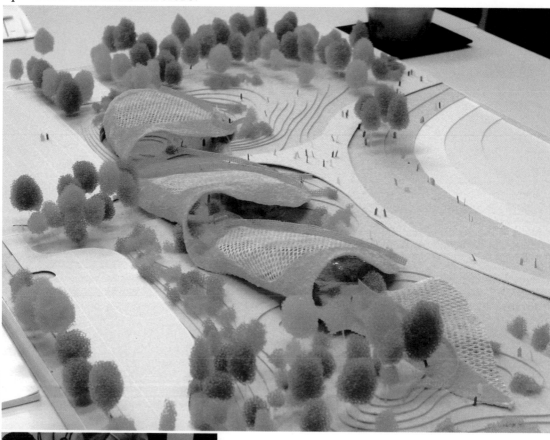

The secondary steel structures cover the openings functioning as skylights around the middle of the shell. The geometry of the roof's main structure is investigated and defined as the optimum structural shape that minimizes the strain energy and deformation through the operation of modifying the initial shape the architect imaged by means of shape analysis based on sensitivity analysis method.

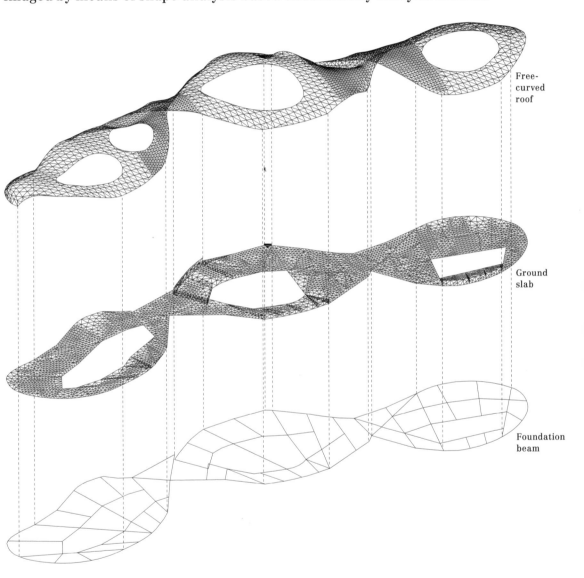

Free-curved roof

Ground slab

Foundation beam

Model with initial geometry drawn by architect

In the meantime, as a basic study, this 190 m-long element was treated as symmetrical, so the shape was determined using a half-model. A thickness of 40 cm was established using this initial shape. As this is also a free-curved surface, compression, tension and bending stresses were all generated.

Evolutionary process of the shape alteration (40 cm thickness).

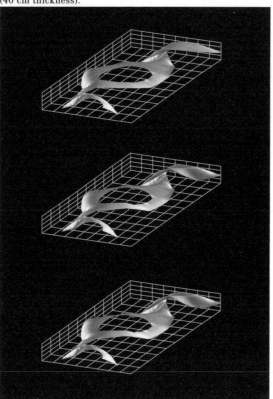

These figures also show the reduction of maximum displacement and strain energy with each evolutionary step.

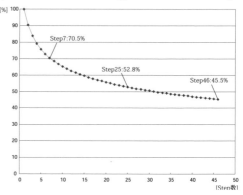

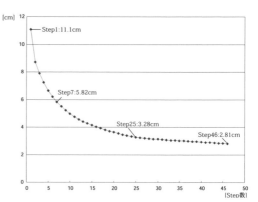

The process by which the cross-section changes at each roof position

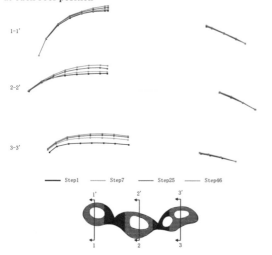

This is an insufficiently rational shape in mechanical terms, so at the first step the maximum transformation is in the vicinity of 2 m. The evolution ultimately converged around the dashed lines, and the final shape was satisfactory in terms of design as well as mechanics. The transformations from the initial shape up to this point initially yielded a maximum displacement of 14 cm. This finally became 2 cm as it evolved toward a high-rigidity shell.

The green roof enables the building to merge into the surrounding landscape and allows people to walk on it. With soil, vegetation and the people, it was calculated on the basis of an exceptionally heavy live load of 1.5 t/m².

There is another interesting topic related to this: what would happen if we tried using a thickness of 15 cm instead of 40 cm?

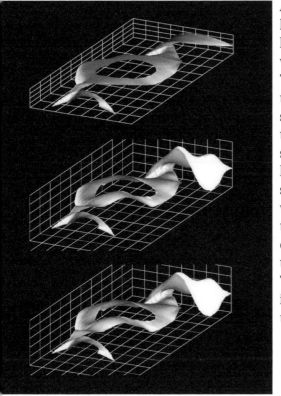

Analysis showed that it would end up like a piece of bacon frying in a pan, leaping about 9 m at the first step, with a maximum displacement of 70 cm. The model itself seemed to be telling us that the architect's arbitrary shape was structurally unsound if it was to be so thin. A thickness of 15 cm becomes possible if the loads are somehow resisted by means of membrane stress, but it also seemed to be asking us if such a shape was acceptable. And in this case, too, the final shell did evolve into a mechanically rational shape with no significant transformations after two steps. This was a very long way from the initially desired form, and not very useful for design purposes.

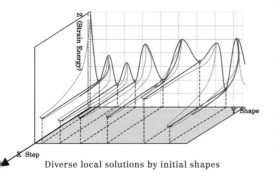

Diverse local solutions by initial shapes

To explain what these drawings are expressing, the X coordinate is the evolutionary step number, the Y coordinate is the local solution group, and the Z coordinate is the strain energy. For example, if you want a shape to converge on a certain local solution, the initial form—that is, the initial value—should be established as close as possible to that local solution. If a different initial value is established, it will converge on a different local solution. As there are many possible local solutions for a non-linear problem, it is necessary to establish a suitable initial value for convergence on a specific target.

Process of shape evolution by the Sensitivity Analysis method
The entire roof was examined by means of shape analysis based on
the structural optimization method with the following assumptions:
- Constrain condition: pin supports where the roof's surface touches the ground
- Material: 40 cm thick concrete
- Dominant load: 1.5 t/m², equally distributed vertical load on the roof

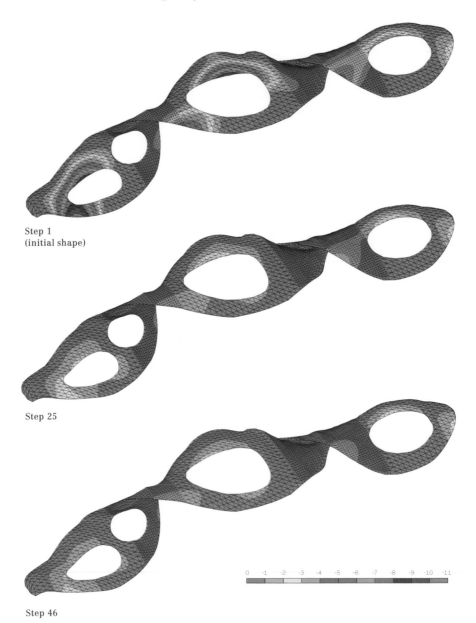

Step 1
(initial shape)

Step 25

Step 46

This shows the sequence of the roof's vertical deformation by the above-mentioned
load condition from the step of the initial shape to the step of the final shape.
As the shape evolves, overall deformation is dramatically reduced.

Process of evolution (section)

The first shape drawn by the architect

The final shape after the analysis

Principal membrane stress

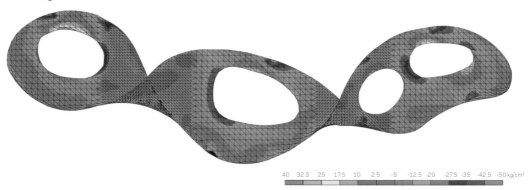

40 32.5 25 17.5 10 2.5 -5 -12.5 -20 -27.5 -35 -42.5 -50 kg/cm²

Principal bending moment

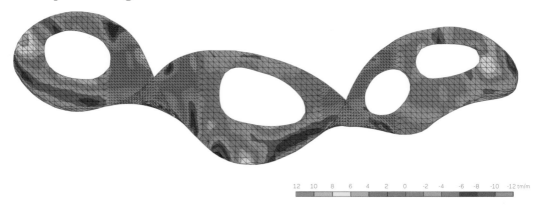

12 10 8 6 4 2 0 -2 -4 -6 -8 -10 -12 tm/m

The structural safety of the final shape obtained by the shape analysis was examined through the ordinary structural analysis method, FEM analysis with commercially available software such as NASTRAN. The figures above show the result of the analysis (principal stress distribution and principal bending moment distribution).

The arrangement of reinforcement is defined according to the result of the analysis. The main reinforcement for the roof uses steel rods with a diameter of 16 mm on account of rational working process at the construction site. The interval of the steel rod is 150 mm and partly 75 mm. Though the direction of the arrangement follows the axis of a common coordinate, some rods are arranged in the direction of the radiation and circumference against the curved surface (in those areas where the geometry of curved surface is complicated).

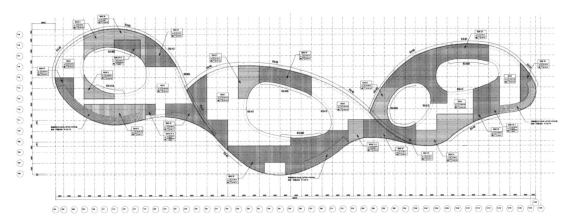

Arrangement of top reinforcement for roof slab

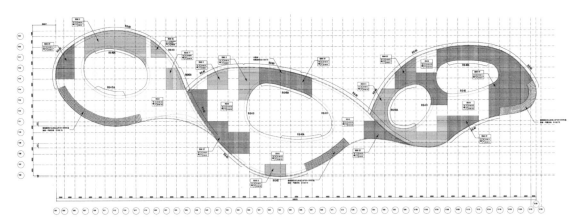

Arrangement of bottom reinforcement for roof slab

There are tie beams (colored in red in the figure below) properly arranged in the substructure so as to deal with the thrust transmitted from the upper structure. These tie beams are essential for the structure to realize the upper shell structure. PC strands with a diameter of 21.8 mm (8 rods, maximum) are arranged in the tie beam and introduce pre-stress. Since the thrust generates tensile stress in the reinforced concrete slab (t=400mm) on the ground level as well, steel rods (19 mm to 25 mm) are arranged in the middle of the section.

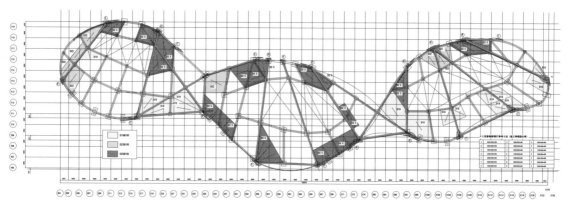

The physical model was remade by Toyo Ito's office on the basis of the shape solutions thus obtained. If laser-forming technology is used, free-curved surfaces can be very smooth in the model, but their actual execution on site is an enormous task.

The number one problem in on-site reinforced concrete construction is complex formwork. At Fukuoka we used a combination of ordinary plywood formwork and steel mesh that functions as formwork, and managed to achieve smooth free-curved reinforced concrete shells. The plywood framework was cut into 1 x 2 m (partly 1 x 4 m or 1 x 1 m) pieces and transported to the site. The panels were joined very precisely to make a smooth curve. About 2000 m³ of concrete was cast by 400 workers. The operation was very difficult because there were no flat slabs and the reinforcing bars were very densely arranged.

1 Formwork at Gringrin
2 The arrangement of reinforcing rod for shell
3 Concrete casting

Exterior view

Interior views

Kakamigahara Crematorium

Toyo Ito, 2004–2006

The Crematorium in Kakamigahara is another free-curved surface shell produced
in collaboration with Toyo Ito. This photo shows the 3D model produced using the
same procedure as for Gringrin. As explained in that case, a smooth free curved
surface is easy to make at the scale of a model, using the 3D data obtained by the
shape analysis, but realizing it on site is extremely difficult.
We should note that the construction materials currently available to us range
from steel, concrete and timber to FRP and carbon fibre. We have to select
the most rational materials and construction methods from among these, but we
are obliged to use the most economical, safest and most reliable construction
methods. This being so, for the time being I am unable to think of a rational

alternative to the rich plasticity of reinforced concrete shells. Eventually these free curved surface shells were realized using reinforced concrete.

In the case of reinforced concrete construction, the biggest problem is how to manufacture the complex formwork for a real building. Here we started by submitting the 3D data for the desired shape to a formwork fabricator, just as in a model-making process. The fabricator dealt perfectly with the difficult problem by making full use of the 3D CAD/CAM technique and produced a reinforced concrete shell with a smooth free curved surface in a sufficiently rational economical way by combining ordinary plywood formwork and special formwork.

The one-storied building (partially two stories) is composed of the reinforced concrete (RC) bearing wall and the roof—a thin continuous free-curved surface shell like a piece of fabric covering the mass of the building.

The thickness of walls ranges from 200 to 400 mm for bearing walls and from 120 to 200 mm for other walls. These bearing walls, RC columns standing on the walls and some steel posts (Ø 216.3 x 12) randomly arranged along the periphery support the vertical load from the big roof, while the bearing walls withstand horizontal loads such as seismic load and wind load.

The big roof is a free-curved surface shell covering an arbitrary shape (80 m long, 60 m wide and 200 mm thick.) Its geometry is investigated and defined as the optimum structural shape that minimizes the strain energy and deformation through the operation of modifying the initial shape defined by the architect by means of shape analysis based on Sensitivity Analysis method — as the one used in Fukuoka Island City Central Park Gringrin. The analysis produced an extremely light (both visually and physically) and rational roof.

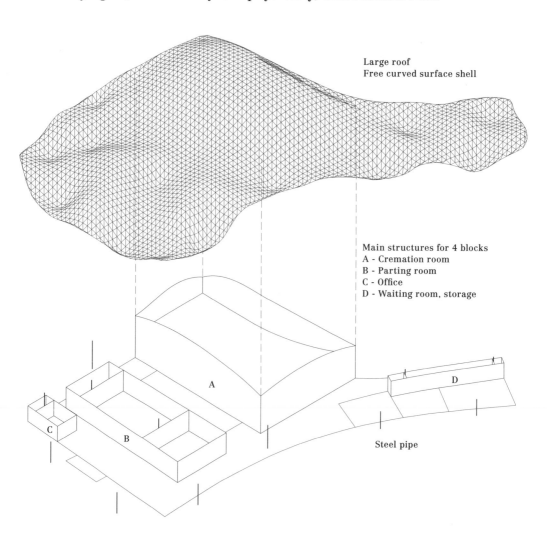

Large roof
Free curved surface shell

Main structures for 4 blocks
A - Cremation room
B - Parting room
C - Office
D - Waiting room, storage

Steel pipe

In the Structural Optimization method, triangulated shell-elements following the one-meter grid compose the model for the shape analysis.

Constrain condition: Columns as roller supports withstanding only vertical load along the periphery. Walls and other columns as pin supports withstanding horizontal loads.
Dominant load: 6.0 KN/m², equally distributed vertical load on the roof.
This is the sequence of the roof's vertical deformation by the above-mentioned load condition from the step of the initial shape to the step of the final shape.
It illustrates that the shape-evolution process dramatically reduces the amount of deformation.

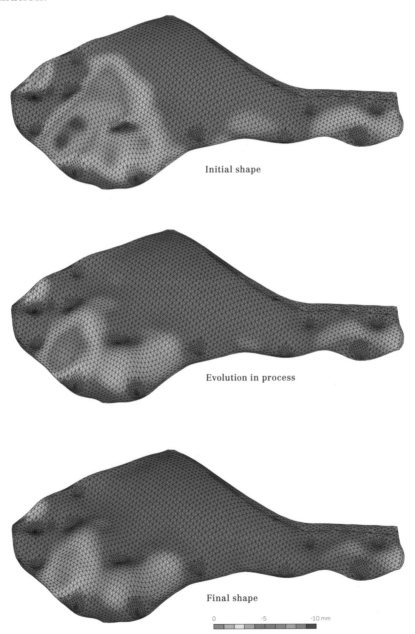

Initial shape

Evolution in process

Final shape

0   -5   -10 mm

The structural safety of the final shape obtained by the shape analysis was examined through the ordinary FEM structural analysis method, using commercially available software such as NASTRAN. These figures show the result of the analysis.

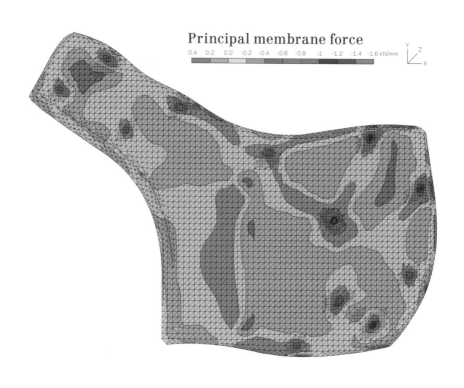

Principal membrane force

0.4 0.2 0.0 -0.2 -0.4 -0.6 -0.8 -1 -1.2 -1.4 -1.6 kN/mm

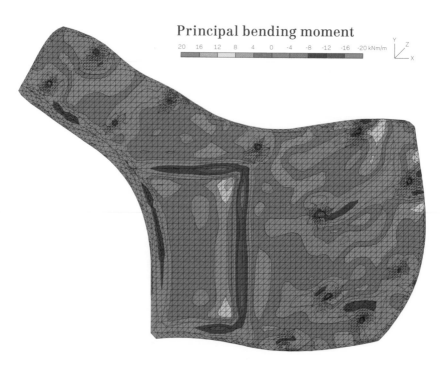

Principal bending moment

20 16 12 8 4 0 -4 -8 -12 -16 -20 kNm/m

The arrangement of reinforcement is defined according to the results of the analysis. A deformed steel rod with small diameter (13 mm) was used for the roof's reinforcement so as to be easily arranged along its undulating curved surface with various curvatures.

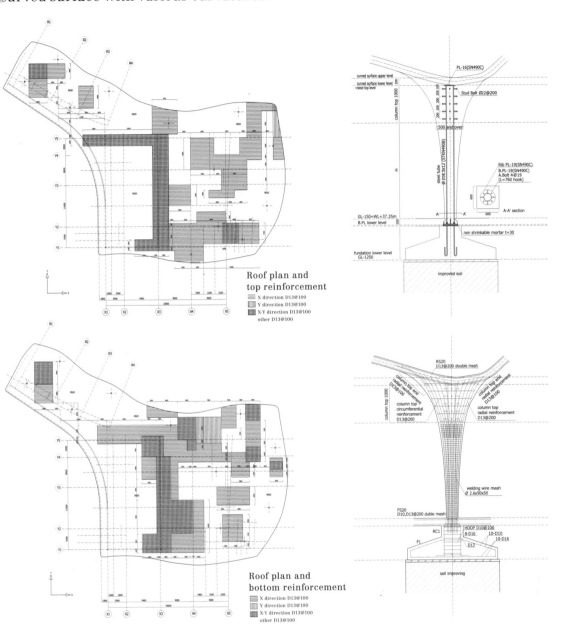

Roof plan and top reinforcement

  X direction D13@100
  Y direction D13@100
  X-Y direction D13@100
  other D13@100

Roof plan and bottom reinforcement

  X direction D13@100
  Y direction D13@100
  X-Y direction D13@100
  other D13@100

This shell had a thickness of 20 cm, and had no sort of plants on top. The shape had to have a much smoother finish than the Fukuoka project. The fabricator thus made special frameworks using CAD/CAM, and to support the plywood formwork large wooden beams were placed at intervals of 1 metre, with smaller beams every 25 cm. In addition, special formwork was used at the more curving points. The result was an extremely smooth surface.

Photographs of shell formwork and arrangement of reinforcing rods

In addition to compression, the structure of a free-curved shell must also accommodate a degree of tension and bending stress. In order to avoid the loss of rigidity due to cracks forming in the concrete, a hybrid construction of steel plates and concrete is ideal from a structural design standpoint. After acting as the concrete formwork during construction, the steel plates are then unified with the concrete in a composite cross-section. However, the likelihood of greatly increased costs unfortunately meant that we were unable to use this method in either the Crematorium project or the Gringrin project.

These panoramic views show the formwork, the arrangement of reinforcing rods and completion of the concrete casting.

The 20 cm thick shell was finished with a perfect free edge, appearing to lightly hover in the air. In practice, people are not allowed onto the roof, but structurally it can bear the load of people walking on it.

2.1 Extended Evolutionary Structure Optimization method (Extended ESO method)
Florence new station
Arata Isozaki, competition proposal, 2003

I would like now to discuss the shape design potential of another new spatial structure, entirely different from these free-curved shells. The subtropical banyan tree has aerial roots braced at several places on the sloping trunk, and manages to support itself on this inclination. The stress level is equalized by the principle of uniform stress, which is implemented by evolving individual shapes—a process guided by the self-organizing capacity of living creatures. These vegetal structures illustrate a mechanism for the production built structures. In 2003, we tested this idea in Arata Isozaki's Florence New Station competition proposal.

The mechanical theory based on this design is the three-dimensional extended evolutionary structural optimization method (Extended ESO method) developed by our laboratory, a mechanical theory which uses von Mises yield stress as a reference value. As will be explained in more detail below, the shape of this flux structure evolved toward uniform stress; in other words, it derives from the same theory as that of the evolution of plant shape. In the mechanical optimization of large-span structures dominated by gravitational loads, digitally evolving the shape so as to minimize the amount of material used in the structure will lead to a mechanically optimum form based on the given design parameters. These parameters include here constraints deriving from the building's functions as well as mechanical conditions such as loads and support points, all of which can be quantitatively described.

This method was applied in the new Florence Station to the design of a structural element with a maximum central span of 150 m between support points. The initial state of the design field is a rectangular volume, 36 m wide x 20 m high x 150 m long, with support points at each end with a lateral separation of 10 m. The architectural constraints on this rectangular volume require the roof surface to be consistently flat, and the lower surface of the central part to be within 12 m of the roof. The dominant load condition was assumed to be w=1t/m^2 uniformly distributed on the roof.

A subtropical banyan tree manages to support itself by bracing the sloping trunk with a number of aerial roots.

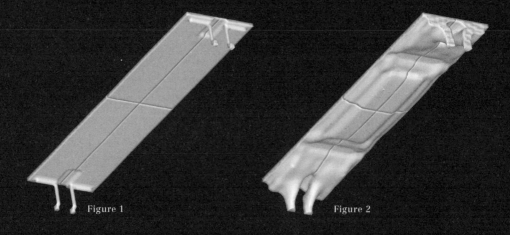

Figure 1

Figure 2

The constraints: the roof must be consistently flat, the lower surface of the central part must to be within 12 m of the roof. The roof plate becomes thicker as stress increases.

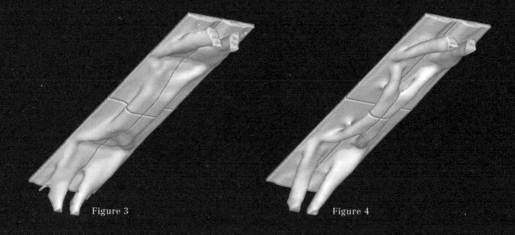

Figure 3

Figure 4

The columns evolve to make an arch-like shape, then mutating into a catenary structure in the centre.

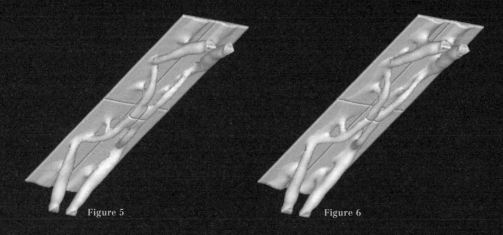

Figure 5

Figure 6

The arch and catenary evolve and fork to support the roof on thinner tubes.

These figures show the results of shape analysis using the extended ESO method. The shape evolution process is shown through successive three-dimensional computer graphic images, from the initial state through to the final evolved state.

In order efficiently to carry out extensive matrix operations using the three dimensional Finite Element Method (FEM) on the rectangular volume that comprises the entire design field, an analysis model was established for the initial state shown in the first figure. Figure 2 shows the evolution of the roof plate structure, in which a large increase in stress has caused the thickness of one part to swell. The shape then undergoes a major evolution as the perpendicular support elements at either end begin to incline three-dimensionally in an arch-like shape. Figure 3 shows a catenary structural element beginning to materialize, detaching itself from the roof surface in the centre of the span, as the entire structure evolves toward a structural shape that can resist axial forces. Put in simpler terms, this could be interpreted at the macroscopic level as an evolution into a form that mimics the stress distribution of a continuous beam. In Figure 4, an element connecting the upward-oriented arch to the downward-oriented catenary part begins to evolve. At the same time, part of the arch and the catenary in the vicinity of the connecting point begins to fork so as to reduce the composite stress of the roof structure and the bending stress in the roof element. This shape evolves so as to support the very large 36 m x 150 m roof plate structure more effectively. The central lower surface of the catenary part is almost flat here, on account of the architectural constraint of being within 12 m of the roof surface. Figure 5 shows the shape nearing the end of the evolution; beyond this point, local structure parts are refined by subtle evolutionary changes until they achieve the final stage of evolution as shown in Figure 6.

The bending of the structural elements is minimized throughout the entire structure, with the reference variable of von Mises stress being equally distributed in order to achieve maximum energy transmission efficiency, and obtaining a structurally rational shape without mechanical wastage.

Validation by general structural analysis

The 3D coordinate of this organic structure was already determined by the shape analysis, so we then went on to re-validate the stress deformation and sections of the members by means of a general FEM analysis in order
to demonstrate the safety and mechanical rationality of the resulting structure. The maximum stress of the final structural elements is less than 1.4 tf/cm² (allowable stress, uniformly distributed) and perpendicular displacement in the middle of the span (L = 150 m) is 20 cm (1/750 of L). It is therefore considered safe enough for earthquake and thermal stress conditions.

Extrapolation of 1/4 of the whole model (boundary conditions were considered to be symmetrical)

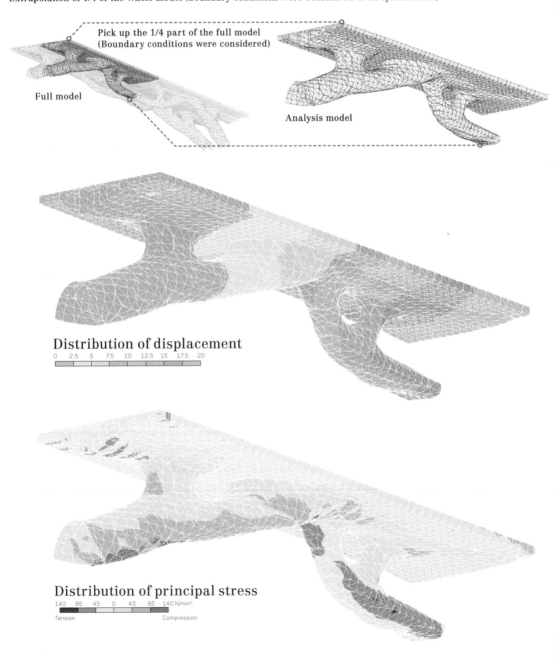

Pick up the 1/4 part of the full model
(Boundary conditions were considered)

Full model

Analysis model

Distribution of displacement

0   2.5   5   7.5   10   12.5   15   17.5   20

Distribution of principal stress

140   95   45   0   45   95   140 N/mm²

Tension   Compression

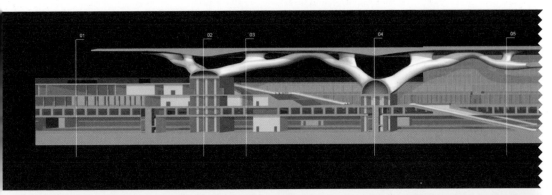

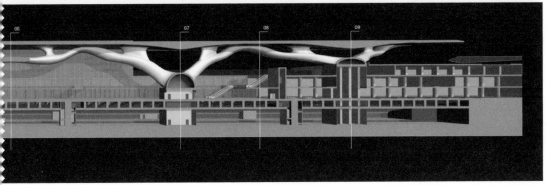

Cross sections

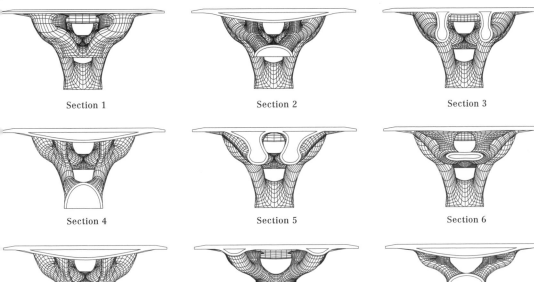

Section 1

Section 2

Section 3

Section 4

Section 5

Section 6

Section 7

Section 8

Section 9

Qatar Education City (QEC)
rata Isozaki, Convention Centre, 2003–

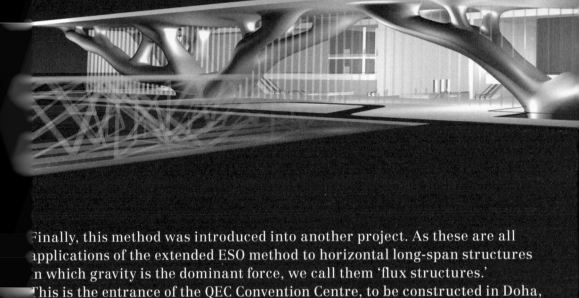

Finally, this method was introduced into another project. As these are all applications of the extended ESO method to horizontal long-span structures n which gravity is the dominant force, we call them 'flux structures.' This is the entrance of the QEC Convention Centre, to be constructed in Doha, Qatar. An enormous structure 25 m long x 30 m wide x 20 m high. The structure has maximum efficiency with a minimum use of material, and the distance between its support points reaches up to 100 metres. It is currently in the construction phase.

By making full use of a man-machine interface, shape design can be described as a design activity incorporating the value judgments of the designers at every stage of the operation. In this case the designers are an architect and an engineer working together. Each has his own area of responsibility: aesthetic value judgments from the architect and mechanical value judgments from the engineer

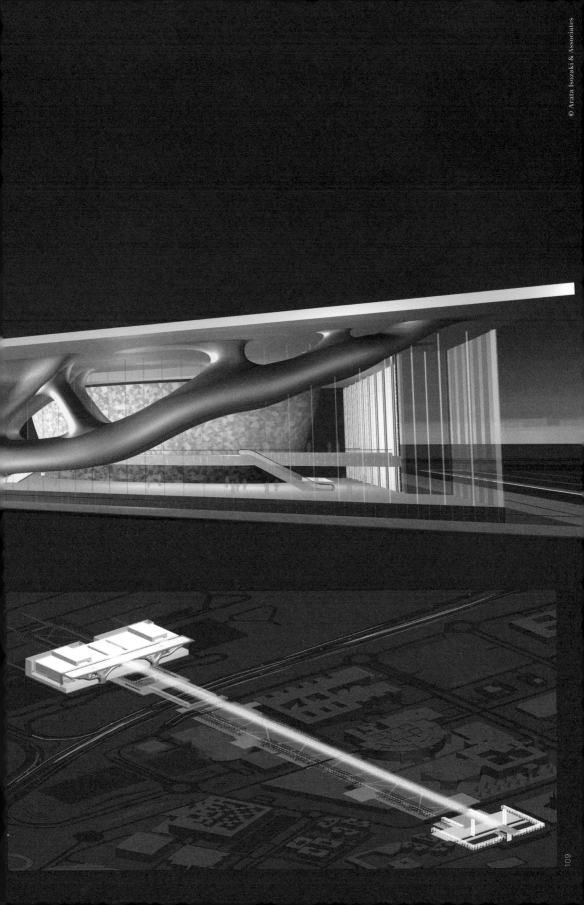

These figures show the stages of shape analysis using the extended ESO method. But after the experience of the Florence Station competition (in which the analysis was undertaken based on the basic conditions—4 columns and a roof), we could now start with the supposition of a final shape. Our starting point in Qatar was a much more advanced structural shape, thus saving ourselves an enormous amount of calculation.

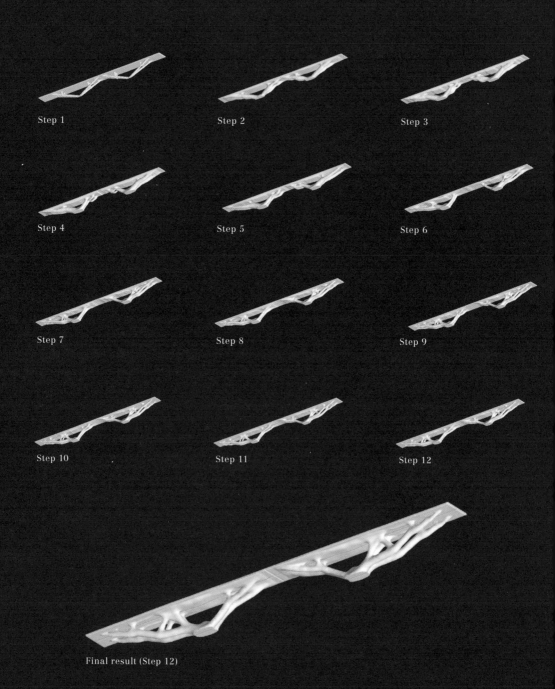

Step 1

Step 2

Step 3

Step 4

Step 5

Step 6

Step 7

Step 8

Step 9

Step 10

Step 11

Step 12

Final result (Step 12)

Construction process

Step 1
Erect trunk portion by
crawler crane

Step 2
Erect temporary supports and
erect branches

Step 3
Continue installation of temporary
supports and erection of branches

Step 4
Install temporary supports
and erect leaf

Step 5
Continue installation of temporary
supports and erection of branches

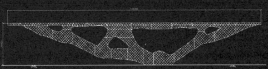

Step 6
Remove temporary supports

Structural diagram

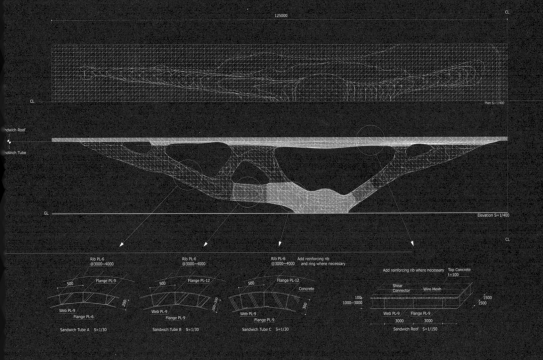

The structural tubes are produced at a factory in Malaysia.

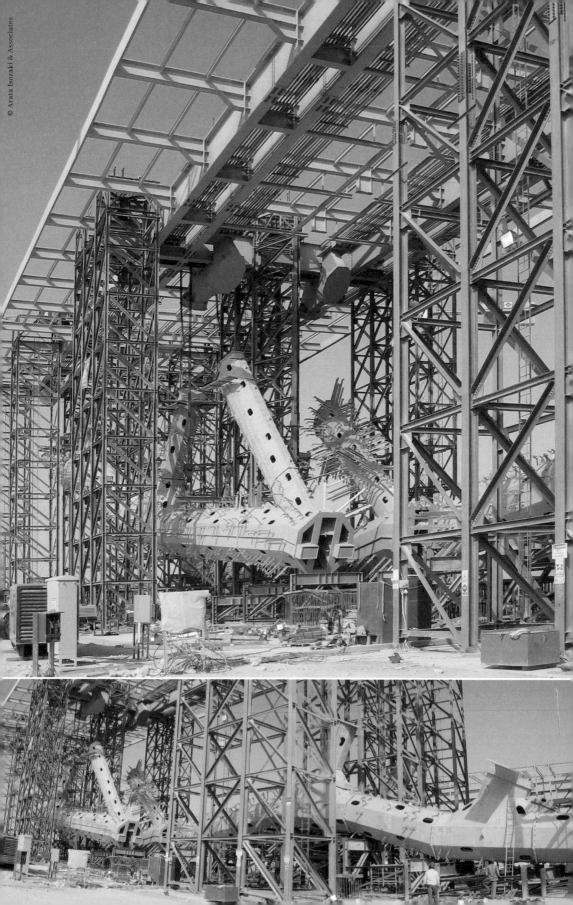

p.art® at Adams Kara Taylor
(parametric applied research team)
is the experimental research team at AKT (Adams Kara Taylor), the design led
Structural and Civil Engineering Consultancy based in London whose driving force is the dialogue with the architect, other designers and the client.
A young professional team with a variety of backgrounds including architecture,
structural analysis, computer science and 3D visualisation and animation, p.art
allows for the intellectual speculation of academia to extend into and redefine
the realm of engineering and architectural practice. **www.akt-uk.com**

p.art work with a diverse range of architects and designers each one employing a different approach to the creative process. At times they are part of a complex web of interacting development stimuli and aesthetic aspirations. At other times interacting sensitively with the spatial experience that an architect or designer is seeking, the complexity possibly not coming from the diverse range of design constraints that must be considered but from the rigorous application a geometrical rule set, material choice or specific design style which must be adhered to.

How can a structural engineering practice adapt its business systems and organisational procedures in such a way that the response to these diverse design requirements is a proactive and collaborative engagement with other designers rather than a passive mechanistic adherence to the traditional design process? The approach at AKT has many strands and, as with all complex systems within business and nature, the optimum performance is only achieved when each strand works in harmony and with fluidity. One of the organisational strands within AKT is p.art, the parametric applied research team.

The aim within p.art is to bring together designers from a variety of backgrounds such as architecture, structural analysis, computer science, forensic analysis, and 3D visualisation and animation. This array of cross disciplinary skills and training is then utilised to find and develop a toolkit of design approaches and methodologies which can be brought to bear on specific project design challenges. Of course each project brings a unique set of design hurdles to overcome, the ongoing question with each project is how best to utilise and develop the toolkit of methodologies in order to customise the process to suit the particular project.

The work within p.art is aimed at developing the discipline of structural engineering, as it is currently perceived by many, towards a more pluralistic approach taking advantage of skills from a range of design disciplines. In the following articles we present some of the work currently being undertaken covering diverse aspects of the design process including:

- Current and proposed use of parametric design software.
- Simplexity: Embedding structural analysis information in the design process.
- Parametric studies of the interaction between global geometry and local
  structural element.
- Student workshops on materiality versus parametric design.

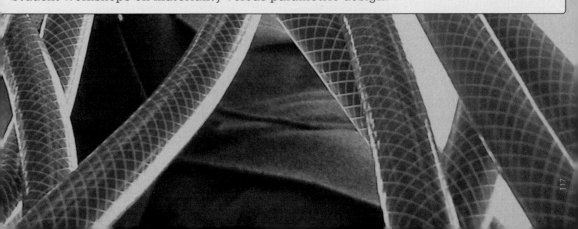

Open systems:
approaching novel parametric domains

Marco Vanucci

Some of the most relevant shifts in contemporary architectural discourse and practice are intrinsically connected with evolution in computation techniques and software development.

The novelty in architectural design brought forward by new computational tools is often related to software packages or digital techniques developed in other design fields. Innovations in computational as well as manufacturing processes, in fact, experimented and developed by naval, aero, automotive and products industries have represented seminal undertakings for innovation in the construction industry and, moreover, for experimentation in architectural practice.

The introduction of parametric software packages in the world of architecture and structural engineering, despite being a fairly new paradigm, is already redefining the discipline from within.

Traditional CAD products create lines, arcs, circles and a great variety of geometrical objects; making design changes to a given geometry requires changing all appropriate components in order to make the drawing correct.

A new generation of parametric design systems establishes models defined by a collection of constrained relationship between objects. In other words it allows setting up parametric geometrical arrangements capable to build anticipated variations between objects.

A parameter is a variable to which other variables are related by means of parametric equations: design modification and creation of a family of component parts can be performed efficiently by setting up reconfigurable smart models capturing the underlying logic of the design.

The instrumentation of parametric setups into architectural practice is starting to shift the role of the architect in the design processes: from the design of specific shapes to the determination of those geometrical / algorithmic relationships describing the project and its components. The design shifts from drawing surfaces to setting up rules of interdependency—genotypes—leading to potential differentiation —phenotypes—.[i]

The novelty represented by parametric tools in architectural culture hasn't found architects unprepared to conceptually understand its potential for contemporary practice: the responsiveness by which architects and advanced design firms gathered the resources of associative design has triggered a fast implementation of parametric tools in the software industry as well as an increasing curiosity to apply its potential in contemporary architectural design.

Nevertheless, despite the receptivity of some of the most interesting cutting-edge architectural practices, it is possible to trace certain tendencies concerning different approaches, some limitations and novel developing scenarios.

Architecture is ultimately characterized by the need for a coherent design logic between different elements forming a whole constituted by an interiority and an exteriority; quality and meaning are achieved through the rigorous determination of all those elements contributing to the interfacing between the different components and the building in its entirety: facades, detailing, proportions, symmetry, modularity just to name a few. Thus, parametric design is important for that: the possibility to establish intricate system of relations between different objects and their properties fusing the hierarchy between parts and whole.

"So far experimental architects have just jumped from top-down determination of parts to bottom-up determination of wholes." Greg Lynn [ii]

What Lynn points out is the delay by which architects have employed parametric design in the development of bottom-up approaches where the determination of components has been prioritized over the design of the whole. This approach has just represented an extreme case. Nevertheless, reshaping the traditional dichotomy between the building and its parts, new digital parametric tools still leave behind some unexpressed potential for contemporary architecture, particularly in relation to the possibility to define highly modulated wholes together with the determination of differentiated components.
In contemporary construction industry, instead, parametric softwares are often employed in design processes of rationalization and post-rationalization where, given a certain project, the answer to specific problems is required to actualize the desired shape [problem-solving approach].

Branching system: the matrix shows parametric variation of the geometry

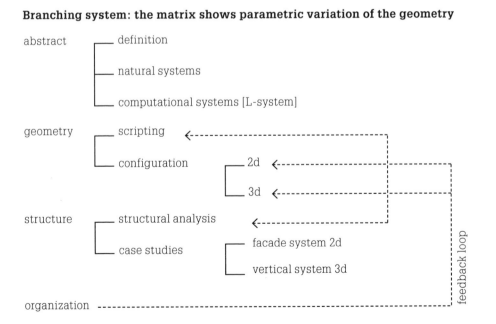

i_Patrick Schumacher – Interview *AJ* 21.12.06
ii_Greg Lynn – *AD Programming cultures*, Wiley Academy, 2006

In this case the potential of computational tools is utilized for its higher degree of precision and speed to deliver tailored ad hoc solutions: the parametric modeling is driven by the need to engineer rational solutions in order to fulfill structural, geometrical or fabrication requirements. In this case, in fact, the potentials for a generative approach are set apart in favour of more pragmatic strategies.

At the other end of the spectrum, by contrast, the proficiency of academic research to implement the generative potential of new computational tools is leading architectural experimentation towards unexplored territories where, more and more often, the figure of the (forthcoming) architect is contiguous to the one of the computer scientist. Thus, academia is quickly pushing the boundaries of parametric/algorhytmic architecture towards the definition of novel paradigms, heading towards a higher level of complexity and sophistication marking an increasing disciplinary divergence between research and practice.

The p.art team sets its line of research at the intersection of these two worlds, searching for the definition of an integral approach to parametric design in the endeavor to bridge the gap between architectural design, structural engineering and evolutionary design strategies. The interdisciplinary structure of p.art and its heterogeneous research spectrum describe an open source design structure where the employment of parametric tools represents one of the most fertile lines of investigation.

p.art is increasingly raising interest within the contemporary architectural and engineering realms due to its capacity to create an innovative interface between architectural research and structural engineering opening up opportunities rather than providing answers. p.art operates allowing collaboration between different disciplines and differing expertise in an attempt to create a common ground where it can be possible to formulate novel design strategies. p.art engages its research agenda through the employment of several different digital tools: among others, parametric software such

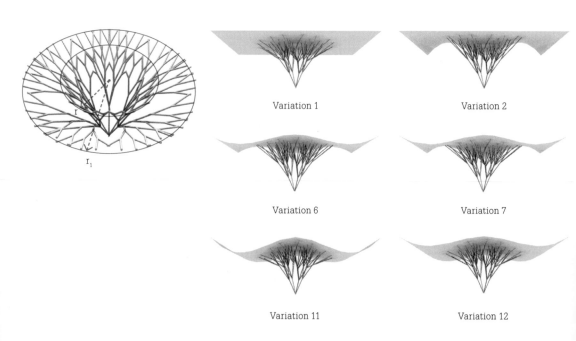

Variation 1   Variation 2

Variation 6   Variation 7

Variation 11   Variation 12

as Digital Project, Gehry Technology's 3D modeling package based on Catia, which it has been used since first the team was set up. The paradigmatic innovation of parametric design originates from its modus operandi: the intrinsic resilience to free-form sketching exercise of Digital Project, in fact, requires a sharper understanding of complex geometry and induces the designer to think through the system logic before even starting to draw a line. In this sense it is projecting desirable perspectives where architectural design is generated from a set of rules and the interdependent relationships between parts governing the manifold aspects of the design. The advent of parameterization increases the complexity of the design task in relation to the necessity to build up not only the model to be designed but also the conceptual structure that guides the parametric variations. From a design point of view it is possible to imagine the advent of design methods based on codified geometrical operations proliferating and interacting to achieve a higher level of complex order: the development of a specific design vocabulary based on parametrically codified instances prefigures a fully integrated design approach where complexity and differentiation emerge from the set-up of coherent and controlled operations.

In this sort of scenario the role of the architect and that of the engineer is contiguous and inform each other in a truly cooperative and generative holistic design process. So far, p.art's engagement with DP is twofold. In the first instance, in fact, p.art's use of DP has been mainly concerned with the study of complex geometry deploying feasible and buildable solutions: it has been deployed in a "problem solving" approach for specific ongoing projects whereby the mutable nature of the design required an adaptive model. The constant adaptation of the structural arrangement to the changing nature of the building envelope throughout the design process allows, among other things, the iterative computation of structural analysis models, almost in real time.

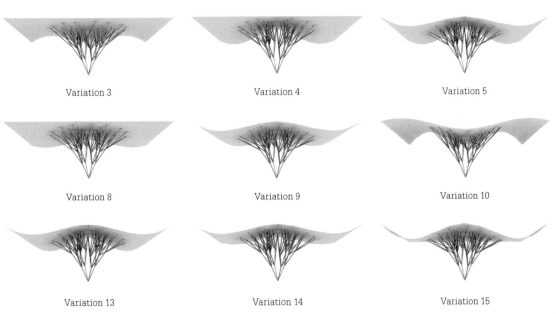

Variation 3   Variation 4   Variation 5

Variation 8   Variation 9   Variation 10

Variation 13   Variation 14   Variation 15

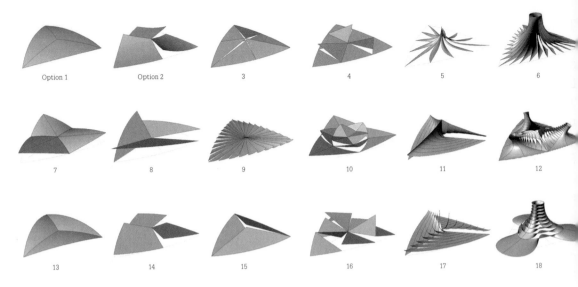

Option 1   Option 2   3   4   5   6

7   8   9   10   11   12

13   14   15   16   17   18

BP Sunbury

Among others, the project for the British Petrol headquarters in Sunbury is an interesting example where parametric modeling has been employed to study the geometrical solution for the roof structure as well as for the delivery of feasible structural system. Numerous geometric arrangements were originally tested to achieve a desirable aesthetic quality and structural viability: the need to provide solar shading to the courtyard below precluded the possibility to utilize translucent lightweight finishes [ETFE]; at the same time, the necessity to provide natural daylight to the suitable levels informed the overall design of the roof and its parts.

By introducing steps within the roof it was possible to introduce vertical glazing through which natural daylight can enter the atrium. The design of the dome shaped roof has been driven by the desire to combine easy fabrication and efficient structural performance. The study of the roof shape has highlighted varying curvature in both lower and higher triangular main panels across the radial directions.

Nonetheless the bespoke triangular panels were extruded from three defined toroids. This allowed identification of planes where structural elements with the same curvature could be defined; in this way, the structure which has been developed presented elements with single curvature for both the lower and the higher roof panels. The structure of the panels was organized between primary beams along the curved edge and secondary beams arranged at 1.5 m spacing perpendicular to the edge ring beams. This methodology created a specific logic around the study of the geometry in order to optimize the fabrication of the elements with identical curvature hence simplifying the fabrication process and increased economy. In turn this methodology allowed easy rationalization of analysis thanks to the selection of few steel sections with similar stress and deflection patterns. The need of fewer number of sections optimized the design time required, providing an efficient result that ease cost saving in the overall design/construction stages of the project.

This type of operation seems, at a first glance, fairly straightforward but it represents a certain level of intricacy in the setting up of the model and its constraints; after a first analysis, in fact, the 3 dimensional model was set up in Digital Project following simple yet rigorous parametric logics.

The main problem concerned the opportunity to establish a simple and efficient set of relationships between parts so that the model could be easily updated in each single geometry as well as in its entirety. The overall geometry of the roof has been simplified and rebuilt starting from the geometrical definition of the toroids to which all other components are related and derived from: indeed, changing the radius of the toroids, the curvature of the roof surfaces are altered determining the adaptation along the surfaces of those lines determining the roof structural beams. This model allowed for reconfiguration of the overall structure and fast adaptation to various and unpredictable design stimuli during the design process (i.e. the need to increase the distance between higher and lower roof surface to increase light penetration).

Traditional program packages— i.e. Rhino—can initially develop quick and precise 3D models; at the same time any occurring change would imply rebuilding the model over and over again until a fixed determination of the design and all its aspects.

Digital Project, on the contrary, despite the more complex and, to a degree, time consuming developmental logic, offers greater advantages: from accommodating unpredictable changes happening during the process to extracting precise data for structural analysis or fabricators.

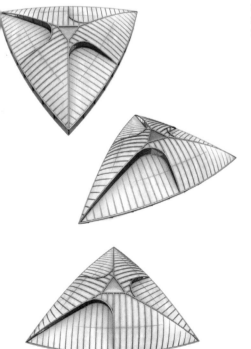

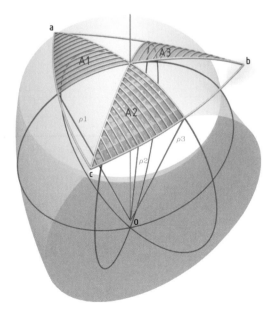

BP Sunbury: the diagram shows the geometrical principle from which the ovel geometry was parametrically generated: three toroids are drawn; the tree geometries forming the roof are sections of the toroids. The angle of curvature of such surfaces is determined by the parametrized length of the radiuses of the toroids.

Branching system:
the matrix shows parametric variation
of the geometry

Levels

Nodes

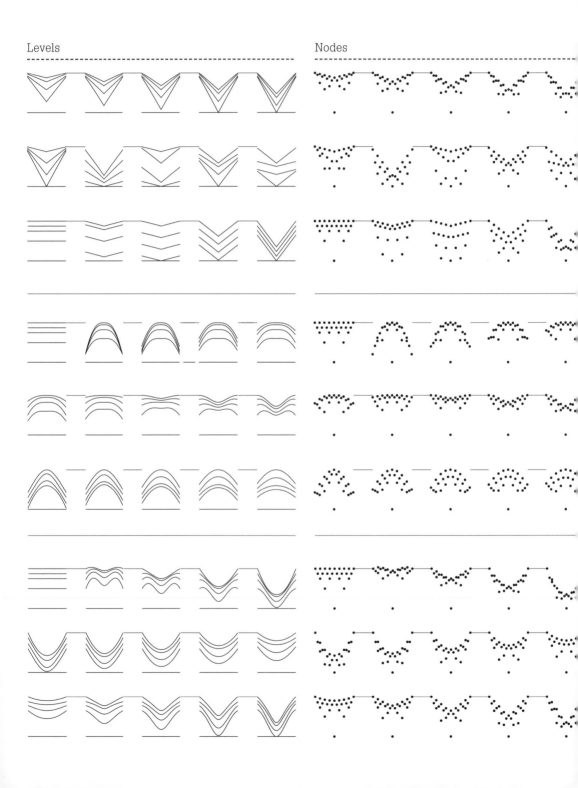

aches

Surfaces

Open system: branching structures

A second approach towards parametric design is represented by the attempt to build up a deeper understanding of structural systems as multi-performative design set-ups. Moving away from the homogeneous standardization of the Modern paradigm, this research, through the generative use of parametric tools, is seeking to investigate open systems as multi-performing, differentiated organizational systems.

In line with the experimentation on branching structures developed by Frei Otto, the research unfolds through a series of exercises aiming to open up a generative approach to parametric design: specificity is achieved through iterative differentiation, adaptation through redundancy, robustness through structural-geometric interdependency. Understanding architectural design as a process of formation leads to the exploration of a pre-material state of given systems: namely, the state prior to the crystallization into a specific design form is explored. In this way, open systems act as virtual machines prior to the actualization into a given design scenario. Methodologically, different paths are followed in an attempt to open up potentials for inclusive performance:

Organizational logic: branching is explored as an organizational system. Different network topologies are analyzed and compared.

Geometrical logic: the geometrical logic of branching is created and developed through parametric tools: Digital project is employed to generate the geometrical structure; in addition differentiation is achieved by the instrumentalization of the defining principle: angle between branches, number of branches, length, displacement of the nodes in space... An intricate matrix is then emerging from the proliferation of differentiated geometrical operation.

Structural logic: the structure and the stability of the various configurations is analyzed through finite element analysis software [FEA]. Thus running structural analysis necessitates specifying a range of parameters to set up likely structural scenarios. Running structural tests on differentiated geometrical arrangements is possible to detect certain general behavioral patterns happening during the process of extracting precise data for structural analysis or fabrication.

The possibility to establish interdependent relationships between different system logics contributes to the redefinition of common fitness criteria: each system logic, instead of responding to a specific optimized scenario, informs each other towards a multi parametric performing whole. Geometrical arrangements, spatial affects, structural performance and organizational logic contribute to the formation of the system and its performance-based logic. p.art develops its research in the endeavor to shift the architectural paradigm from a problem-solving to a problem-caring approach where integral design logics contribute to the coherent employment of novel design method.

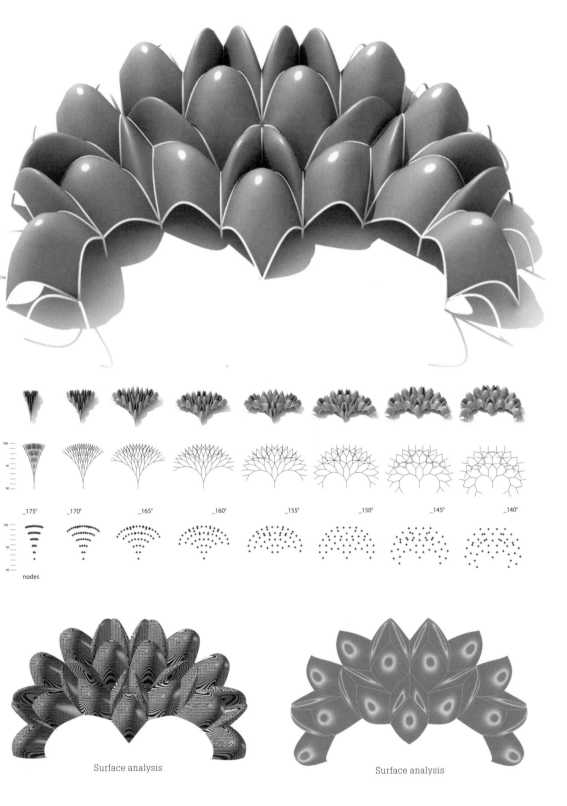

_175°   _170°   _165°   _160°   _155°   _150°   _145°   _140°

nodes

Surface analysis

Surface analysis

Barnsley market roof

The geometry was defined by the architect—it rises at one end by 20m and dips at the other end by 9 metres, both edges cantilevered/angles outwards.

Structural concept of a rib structure fabricated from riveted metal plates. The structure is clad by a single ETFE strip pillow between two ribs. The entire structure is also to be supported by the the adjacent buildings.

The ribs were extracted from the architects model for structural analysis. This enabled us to define limits and constraints to begin refining the geometry of the roof.

Parametric model was set up based on fixed length of roof and heights of either ends and that the roof must be symmetrical. The number of ribs were determined by the standard ETFE span. Alterable factors are the angles of cantilever at each edge, which defines the longest length hence defining the orientation of each plate. We were able to generate several options for analysis.

Through sofistik analysis, it was determined that the maximum angle for the edge cantilever/overhang is 20 degrees. There needs to be a single rib whose orientation was perpendicular to the ground, to ensure structural integrity. Cable ties are to be employed to tie the whole thing together. Calculations also determined minimum plate widths for the ribs.

There are 2 types of ribs, the concave and the convex. It became apparent through analysis that the width at the quarter length point of the rib was more important than supporting ends, due to buckling patterns. With a set of figures as requirements, the next task would be how to accommodate them and develop them into a set of continuous aesthetically logical (and pleasing) steel plate profiles.

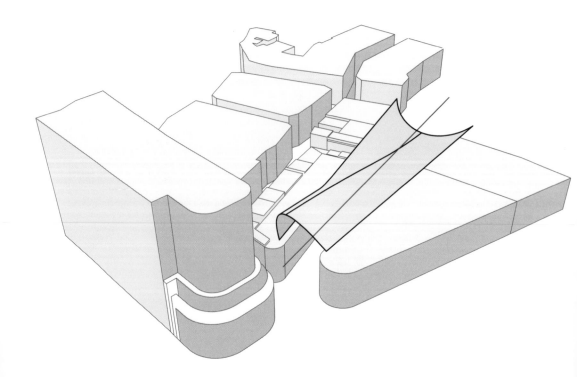

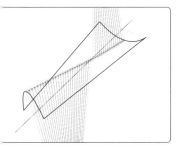

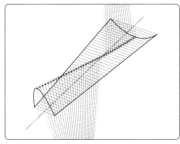

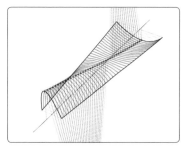

Adhering to spans between 3-3.5 meters to accomodate standardised ETFE panel dimensions, the middle line of the surface was divided longitudinally into 42 segments of equal spans (43 points).

Having established the 43 points on the middle line, the boundaries dictated by the adjacent buildings were also divided into the same number of segments.

All 43 profiles were then extracted from the surface. The geometries were then structurally analysed to determine the dimensions of the structural members.

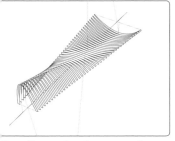

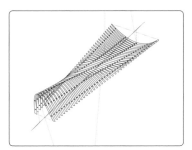

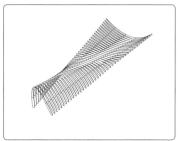

Rib profiles are then drawn according to the sizing provided from the analyses with the material being steel plates.

Points were extracted from each rib for the location of cable ties, all of which were of equal distance along the rib profile.

Each rib plate is then divided into 5 segments of equal length. Each rib is made up of a set of 12 plates which are riveted together; Plates are needed to fix the structure onto the parapets of the adjacent buildings.

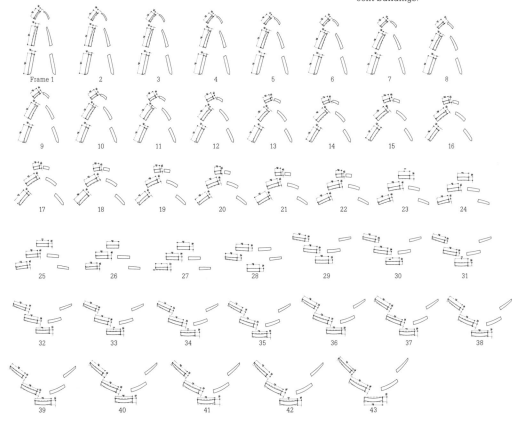

Frame 1 2 3 4 5 6 7 8
9 10 11 12 13 14 15 16
17 18 19 20 21 22 23 24
25 26 27 28 29 30 31
32 33 34 35 36 37 38
39 40 41 42 43

SIMPLEXITY

Sawako Kaijima, Michalatos Panagiotis

Simplexity is a term in system science which describes the emergence of simplicity out of intricate and complex sets of rules.

In recent years there is an increasing trend in architecture to exploit the ability of algorithmic design to produce complex forms by implementing relatively simple and easy formulas. This often results in the addition of unnecessary layers of complexity to a project just for the sake of production of seemingly more complex forms. This in turn can degenerate to computational decoration and after taking into account all the layers of information, the resulting algorithms seem little different than a complicated random number generator.

In contrast there is a whole class of algorithms that deal with simplification which are usually more complex and difficult to implement. This is partly the result of the fact that multiplication and proliferation can be easily implemented via iterative function calls and local simple operations over parts of a system. However, simplification in a way that produces meaningful results and renders the complex system more accessible to human thought and intuition or more efficient is harder to achieve. This is because omitting elements, filtering, reduction, selection and abstraction are procedures that require intelligent and responsible choices as well as some way to refer to and operate on the totality of the system. This implies that the designer needs to have a more or less clear idea as to what she wants to achieve and in addition take full responsibility of the choices made. A deeper understanding of the system on which operations are carried out is required. A lot of these algorithms are hidden within commercial software packages that designers employ in order to realize their projects in the first place. They are the little workers that do not produce spectacular results but guarantee consistency.

Let's take for example an algorithm that iteratively copies a set of points applying some transformation matrix. If the matrix is a contraction this results in the often organic looking Iterated function system imagery. The amount of elements increases exponentially but the algorithm just applies the same transformation mechanically over and over. On the other hand an algorithm that will take a vast amount of points and attempts to reduce them or extract some information like density, shape or skeletal structure will be a rather more complicated story. It will have to scan the totality of the system over and over and then compare, classify, seek spatial relationships like clusters, implied boundaries etc. It will probably require the introduction of more complex data structures both to partition space (e.g. octrees) and to hold derivative elements that describe implied or imposed relationships within the point set (lines, clusters, areas, boundaries etc.). So while the first algorithm only needs to know one type of object, a point as a triplet of numbers, the second algorithm will have to describe points and their relationships using objects of a higher level of complexity.

Another way to see this contradiction is through decision paths. A proliferation algorithm will try to follow all possible paths and avoid making any choice between them. A simplification algorithm will try to find a single more or less optimal path within the constraints of the problem. This implies also that the second requires a well defined problem and hence a better understanding of both the problem and the algorithm's behaviour on the part of the designer.

As we will demonstrate in the following examples simplexity is not just a simplification of form. The simple might arise in different invisible layers of the design and formal regularity (repetitiveness, symmetries, etc.) might actually decline as a result of the application of such algorithms.

Another point we will try to make is that simplexity algorithms are not only employed in the post processing of a given geometric object (rationalization, quantization etc.) but also can be the generating mechanism as well.

Design aspects

From the perspective of the application of computational techniques in design and within an engineering firm we can observe that we are always presented not with whole projects but aspects of them. The involvement into fragments of projects often means that one has to carry out similar operations on different projects. One example of such a cross cutting concern we are going to present is discretization where a project is presented as a continuous manifold and has to be converted to a frame solution or cladding solution taking into account different manufacturing, design and engineering considerations. In the following pages we will present a series of methodologies and the corresponding software tools developed. As the diagram shows below we start with discretization which is a cross cutting concern and appears in a host of projects hence lending itself to generalization. Next we will present a case study of a combination of discretization and optimization within a single project. The third section is concerned with development of a tool by which one can setup an initial environment for a project by placing constraints and design intentions in the form of vector field affectors. Finally we present a project that integrates tools and techniques developed in other projects in order to reconstruct a sense of totality of the project out of its fragments, trying to combine design engineering and manufacturing concerns through computation.

Fields

A recurring theme in the following pages is the field. Fields are mathematical objects defined over manifolds (be it a surface or a 3D portion of space) which enrich these manifolds with spatially varying properties. The introduction of fields allows for a treatment of space as non homogeneous and non isotropic. They help us establish a spatial condition which is variable and multidimensional. Many problems can be raised temporarily to this higher level of complexity and then tools can be used to interrogate the structure and topology of the constructed fields (degenerate points, seperatrices etc.) in order to reach some simpler design solution.

Overview of the work flow

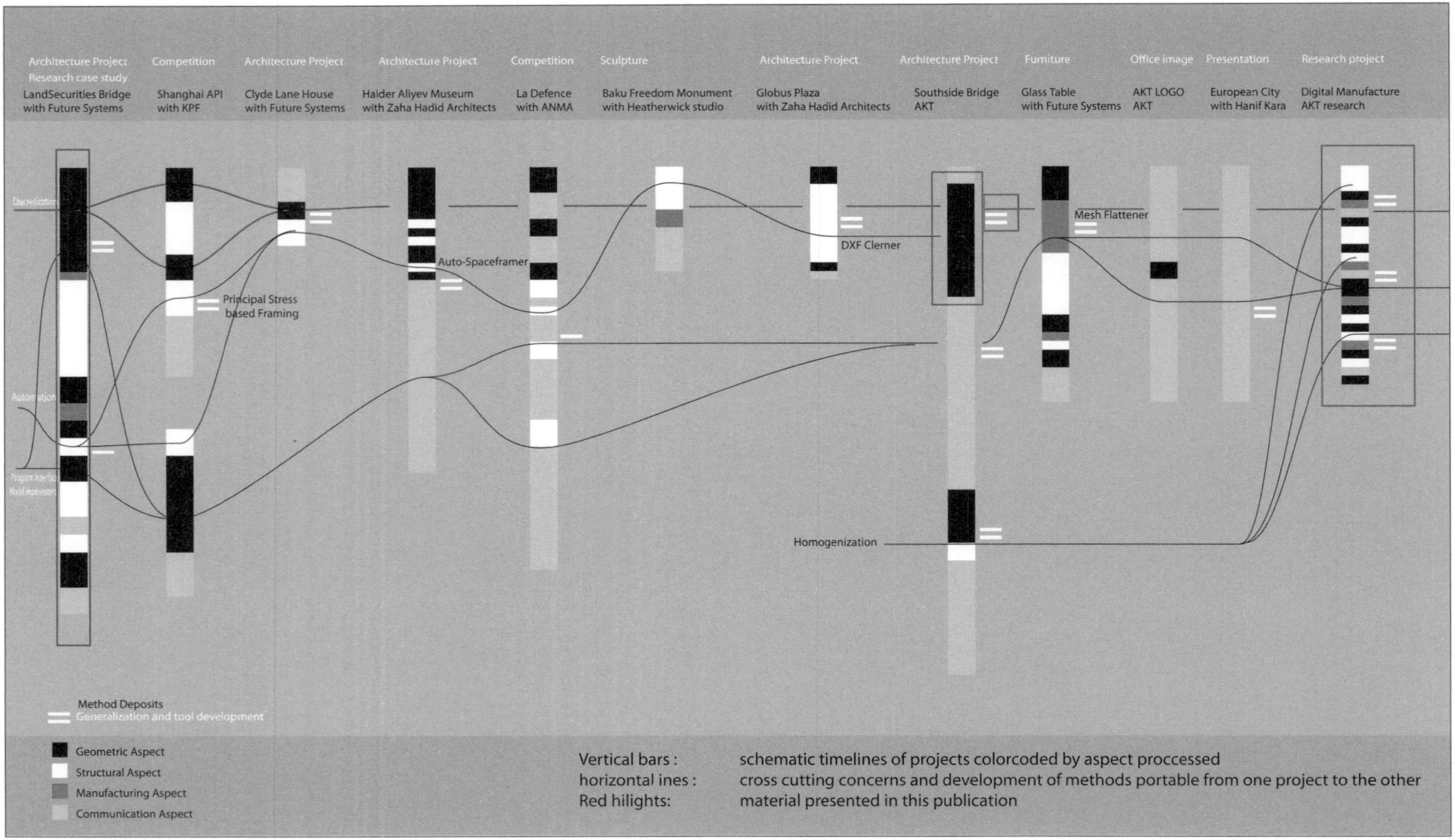

Vertical bars :   schematic timelines of projects colorcoded by aspect proccessed
horizontal ines :   cross cutting concerns and development of methods portable from one project to the other
Red hilights: material presented in this publication

Method Deposits
Generalization and tool development

Geometric Aspect
Structural Aspect
Manufacturing Aspect
Communication Aspect

Architecture Project Research case study	Competition	Architecture Project	Architecture Project	Competition	Sculpture	Architecture Project	Architecture Project	Furniture	Office Image	Presentation	Research project
LandSecurities Bridge with Future Systems	Shanghai API with KPF	Clyde Lane House with Future Systems	Haider Aliyev Museum with Zaha Hadid Architects	La Defence with ANMA	Baku Freedom Monument with Heatherwick studio	Globus Plaza with Zaha Hadid Architects	Southside Bridge AKT	Glass Table with Future Systems	AKT LOGO AKT	European City with Hanif Kara	Digital Manufacture AKT research

Digitalization

Automation

Hyperinterface
Multiframer

Principal Stress based Framing

Auto-Spaceframer

DXF Clerner

Mesh Flattener

Homogenization

1. The circle

The circle was a small program that we were developing for fun while experimenting with particle systems. At that point we stumbled upon the concept of simplexity even before we knew this term existed. The particle system is composed of thousands of particles moving within a force field. Given time all the particles will converge to a single perfect circle at the point where attractive and centrifugal forces balance. Of course you can draw a circle directly by plotting its parametric equation or by any other optimal algorithm well studied in the field of computer graphics. However this is not just any circle but it has a strong connection to the whole system that generated it. The radius of this circle tells something about the underlying force field in a very direct way.

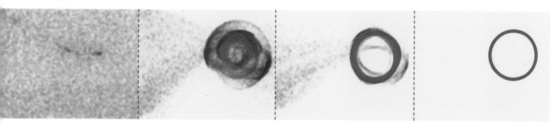

2. Discretization (continuity discontinuity)

A problem that persists in the interface or gap between architecture and engineering practice is discretization. By this we mean the necessity to decompose continuous geometric objects into discrete elements. This is something that is done anyway in visualization programs and FEM analysis packages with each employing algorithms to fit its own set of requirements (well behaved quad element meshes under a given analysis algorithm or minimization of number of facets for visualization purposes). We are concerned with discretization as a design process which takes a continuous domain and lays down elements over which an engineering solution can be built.

One particular case of discretization is when given a continuous smooth manifold as the ones that are mass produced with the proliferation of software based on free form modelling. For the engineers it is often necessary to generate a discrete graph over this manifold, a wireframe model that could suggest ribs of a shell, or a three dimensional frame structure etc. There are many ways to achieve this of course with the most often employed is operating in the ambient space of the given object and partitioning it accordingly (e.g. projecting a grid on a given surface, where the grid is not intrinsically linked to the surface's geometry).

We present here some attempts at developing software tools for interactively interrogating the surfaces in order to construct framing solutions that express intrinsic properties of the given surface. We try to achieve results that look a little less forced and reduce clashes with the underlying geometry.

For demonstration purposes we will use a case study shell. We also make 4 variations of different support conditions for this shell (support at intersection with the ground, linear support along the median axis, dual cores and single big core).

Perspective view of a case study shell

The basic types of first order 2D degenerate tensors

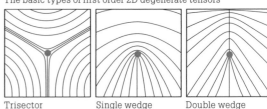

Trisector   Single wedge   Double wedge

Option 1: Rank

For this method we took the advice of engineer Oliver Bruckermann who suggested that a starting point for figuring out a framing solution might be to try to align members with the principal stress directions. So as a starting point we analyze a given surface as if it was a shell with given boundary conditions and then use custom software to selectively extract the stress tensor's streamlines. From the network of curves we can detect the singular points which can be used as guides in the development of a framing solution.

Option 2: Rank

Using scalar fields defined over the given surface. Scalar fields are particularly attractive because they are easy to define and manipulate in real time as well as superimpose using techniques with which many people are familiar through image processing programms. In the above example we chose a scalar field which is intrinsically linked to the geometry and is the distance map.
The distance map assigns a distance value at every point on a surface according to its geodesic distance from the closest boundary edge.

Option 3: Rank

Another intrinsic tensor field to the surface is its curvature field. The streamlines are aligned with the two principal curvature directions and it gives rise to natural looking networks of curves on the surface. Singular points and curves arise in the areas where $H^2+K=0$ that is where the surface is locally spherical.

Option 4: Mapping

In the cases where a surface is given as a NURBS we can use its parameter space to produce tilings. These tilings can be further optimized by using some iterative algorithm in order to meet different criteria. By desribing these criteria as a vector field over the surface we can very easily superimpose them. Such criteria might have a manufacturing or cost effect (making elements similar sizes) or as we will see in the next example (the land securities bridge) might have structural requirements (contractions near areas of high stress).

Plan view and support conditions

Principal stress streamlines under self weight

Extraction of framing lines from stress line diagram

Extraction of framing solution from the distance map field

3. Densification field
(The land securities bridge case)

Continuing on the previous theme of discretization we now present a related real project. The case study of the Land Securities Bridge was developed by focusing on the feasibility study undertaken by Adams Kara Taylor in supporting the design concept by Future Systems for Land Securities. The Land Securities Bridge is designed as a free-form envelope that twists around a pair of paths connecting two floors of the office buildings with a hexagonal mesh forming its cladding system. The complex structure is realized as a lattice of nodes and struts supporting light weight polycarbonate panels. Guidance from the fabrication industry suggested that the number of nodes in the frame would be the biggest cost factor, as the connections will be fabricated one by one, welding a machined spherical piece to standard cut tubes.

From observing the geometry, one could easily understand that all the members of the frame are acting differently from one another due to the complex bridge-form. However, during the structural analysis of the model the majority of the analysis results are ignored in favour of a few singular values which resulted in applying more or less constant cross sections to the whole structure. Even though this type of simplification is one of the most conventional operations when designing a structure, in the case of a non-rectilinear design, we can identify that this approach often leads to over structuring of the form as well as clashes with the geometry and the architectural intentions behind it. The "densification" process was implemented as an attempt to optimize the structural solution within its constraints (hexagonal tiling of constant number of nodes over given skin). At first glance, it seems that this has little to do with simplexity since the end results have a higher diversity of panel sizes and shapes than the original more regular mesh. However the algorithm basically operates on the stress distribution diagram within the parametric space of the surface. The emergent irregularity of the mesh is a reaction to the algorithms attempt to simplify and equalize the stress diagram.

Input

The skin was provided by the architects as a twisting NURBS surface and the hexonal pattern was specified to be the structural framework. The conversation with the fabricator informed us that the number of nodes would decide the construction cost to a large extent. Therefore, we chose an approach that tries to introduce small changes in the structural frame that would improve its structural performance and conformity to the envelope's geometry respecting the inputs.

1 Tiling of the parametric space of the surface

Finite element analysis

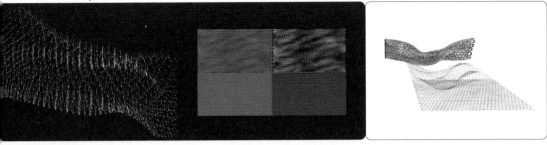

Stress distribution

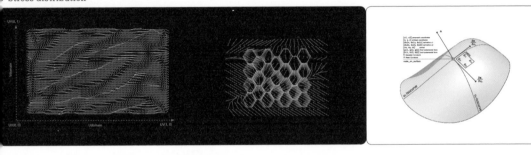

Pattern densification using the stress distribution

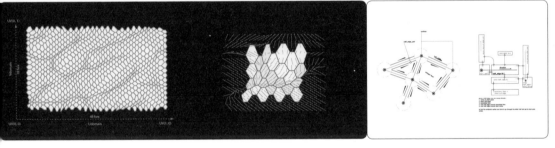

5 Evaluation

The performance and the esthetics was evaluated in each step and if the result was not satisfactory, we repeated the process from the step 2 FEM analysis.

6 Generalization

After the case study, we focused our effort on generalizing the process and made an integrated software tool that allows us to explore the same process for any given surface. We also considered using other patterns, flattening the cladding elements by introducing triangles in the pattern. In addition along with the gradient of the stress field used for the densification, other force fields can be superimposed that drive the geometry towards different goals (e.g. equalization of member lengths, areas or angles) and all these requirements can be superimposed to achieve a compromise between them.

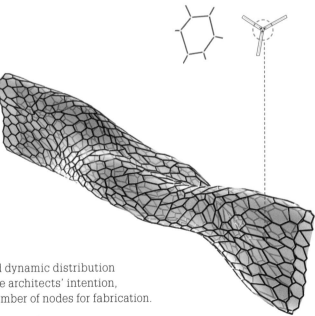

Output

The resultant form shows a more organic and dynamic distribution of hexagonal patterns, that is more true to the architects' intention, with simpler stress distribution and same number of nodes for fabrication.

4. Constructing fields (Field designer tool)

The field designer project challenges the form generating process using digital computation, which initially was conceived as a tool development to help us design a pedestrian bridge over a highway.

Generally, architectural design starts from generating a form and then it is slowly developed to meet the complex design considerations and requirements. However, in this project we present a process that allow us to evolve design without preconditioning the outcome by formal biases.

In most design interfaces, the space is considered homogeneous and isotropic where as in reality and in a design space it is not (e.g. gravity, area of interests). The idea for us was to generate a vector field that the designer could affect and calibrate according to the design intentions and project constraints, thus the design space would be treated non-homogeneous and anisotropic. As an affecter of the field, we developed elements that attract or repulse the field representing primary view point or areas that need to be cleared. We also developed functions to regulate the transition of the field, which, for example, accommodates the inclination requirements for the bridge. To reduce the complexity, we introduced trajectory generators within the field which renders more tangible paths and allow us to detect boundaries within the field. These intermediate bundles of point strings are not fixed to a single representation and can be interpreted in multiple ways. As a result, we are able to generate geometries from the field that is sculpted by multiple considerations related to the design project.

Simplified software structure

The user can move around and manipulate the properties of different types of field affectors. In this diagram we show the types of field affectors and the kind of field they generate.

Classes and properties

Field affector
Point

Line

Directional line

Plane

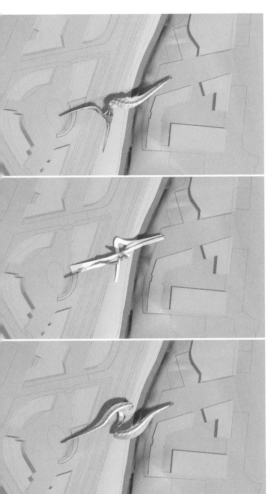

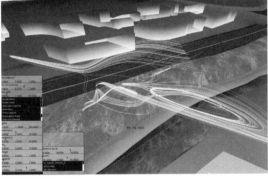

Input of problem description as field affectors—
case study—bridge.

Screenshot from the version of the software developed for the
Southside bridge project.

Variations and selection

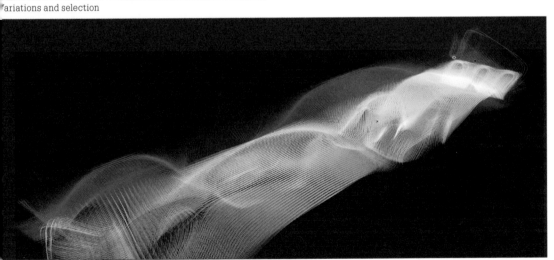

Constructing a material density and stress field according to the method described in the next section where the selected
trajectories become applied loads within the material volume

5. Constructing and interrogating the stress tensor field. Digital manufacturing

Our aim in this ongoing project is to construct a methodology for design developing an integrated software tool in parallel that will allow us to combine structural and manufacturing information with design intentions. As a case study we took to design a light support, however the same methods and software tools developed can be extended to handle larger and more complex projects. In agreement with previous examples we first establish a tensor field over a region of space from which we can gather information to aid us in our design. We want this field to reflect the materiality of the result and chosen manufacturing technique, yet still be indeterminate enough not to imply a singular solution. For this reason, we chose to construct the field out of the simplest known conditions, that is the outer material boundary, the support conditions, and the position of the light bulb and shade that appear as applied loads. From these conditions, we can construct a volume of variable material density endowed with a stress field, which yields a variable coordinate system at each point within the volume. To do that we used a variant of the well documented homogenization method. This is a method which is very elegant in its simplicity. One starts with the assumption of a volume of material with arbitrarily placed loads and supports. Then iteratively we analyze and reassign material densities in the volume until some desired convergence has been achieved.

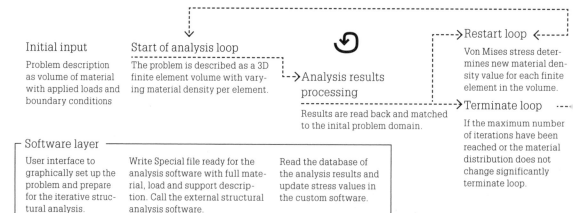

Initial input

Problem description as volume of material with applied loads and boundary conditions

Start of analysis loop

The problem is described as a 3D finite element volume with varying material density per element.

Analysis results processing

Results are read back and matched to the inital problem domain.

Restart loop

Von Mises stress determines new material density value for each finite element in the volume.

Terminate loop

If the maximum number of iterations have been reached or the material distribution does not change significantly terminate loop.

Software layer

User interface to graphically set up the problem and prepare for the iterative structural analysis.

Write Special file ready for the analysis software with full material, load and support description. Call the external structural analysis software.

Read the database of the analysis results and update stress values in the custom software.

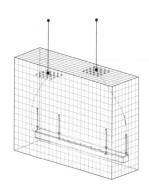

Initial input of problem description

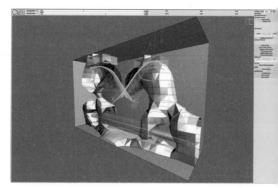

Screenshot of software interface

To start the project we developed a software interface where we can interactively describe the domain of the problem whose parameters include resolution of voxels, dimensions, supports and placement of lights in the form of concentrated load. The software automatically builds a file compatible with the structural analysis program we used (in this case sofistik) and goes through the iterations required. In the end, it allows the extraction of level set surfaces of the Von Mises stress field or selective extraction of the streamlines of the stress tensor field. The interface allows the designer to develop a tactile relation to the field and consequently an intuition of the material behaviour by interrogating the conditions around specific locations.
For the particular object presented here we placed the supports at the top of the volume as the light will be hanging. Applied loads are generated at the endpoints of the hypothetical light location and the light-shade's support points.
By observing, an overview of the field we can see that as expected the major stress direction traces curves roughly linking supports to loads forming nearly vertical bundles. The minor stress direction is predominantly in compression and its absolute value is small relative to the major stress's absolute. Excluding the regions around singularities, it tends to form rings wrapping around the major direction's bundles. Another feature of the bundles of the major principal stress direction is that they form two distinct groups: an outer one wrapping around supports and light-shade support points

---> Interrogation of the results ------> Design decision ------------------> Manufacture

Try to understand the behaviour of the material in the initial volume and suggest solutions. Custom software helps the designer develope an intuitive relation to the behaviour of the field. Design intentions are fed back to the software as new features.

After deciding a general configuration use information from the inital field for every decision. Every direction, every pattern density, and every thickness is extracted from the inital field thus investing with some consistency the final result.

Send information to manufacturer of chosen material and method.

Software layer ——————

Custom software allows visualization of local and global properties of the material and stress distribution in real time. The designer can interactively extract bundles of principal stress streamlines or patterns whose density reflects the material density suggested by the underlying field. As the software was developed in parallel to the project new ideas and possibilities of interpretation of the tensor field were implemented gradually as features or classes of parametric objects.

Generate appropriate files for the chosen manufacturing method, taking into account tolerances and other constraints.

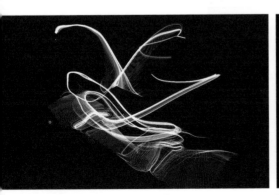

Selective extraction of streamline bundles

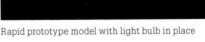

Rapid prototype model with light bulb in place

and an inner structure connecting the supports to the light bulb ends. Because of the slightly asymmetrical placement of the slightly asymmetrical placement of the supports, the whole field is twisting and as a result, this twist is passed to all the elements extracted from it. This meant that we were able to achieve a rather complex distribution of elements that balances itself in space.

What we try to achieve through our approach is design consistency rather than structural optimization strictly speaking.

This consistency is achieved by interrogating a single field for all design decisions. We chose not to discard the designer's intuition in favour of an automaton style algorithm but to embrace it at variable stages. Algorithms are still operational and necessary in many stages of the process and their development was an integral part of our approach but their parameters are exposed through interfaces for the designer to make the most of the information present in the field. What the stress field did is generate a space within which to carry the design that in contrast to most commercial software is neither homogeneous nor isotropic but finite. So instead of starting the design process in a tabula rasa of a Cartesian system one is thrown in a finite volume of variable density where at every point a different Cartesian system defined by the three principal stress directions is bound. What is "parametric" is not the object to be designed itself but the space in which objects are embedded and informed.

The upper element is extracted from stream-lines of the minor stress direction connecting the two support regions. The element helps to shape the cables and its middle part acts in compression.

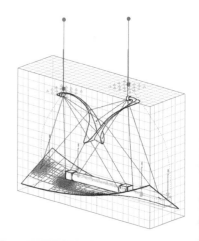

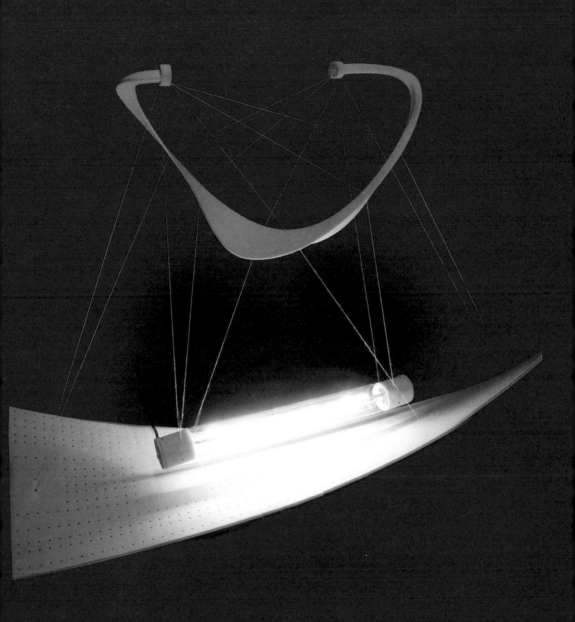

The cables are extracted from streamlines of the major stress direction. The design decision was to use steel wire rope as most of the plastics used in rapid prototyping are brittle and do not work well in tension. There is a single wire which weaves through all the elements (top arc, lamp caps, shade) rendering the need for manual balancing and micro-adjustments in wire lengths redundant. At the tips of the compression arc there are special elements with three holes each to help lock the wire in place. As suggested by the topology of the streamlines an outer loop supports the shade and an inner loop, the light itself.

The bottom shade is composed of three layers measuring roughly 1mm in thickness each. The bottom one is completely solid and the top one has a more or less regular perforation pattern. The middle layer however reflects the material density of the analyzed field in the form of a variable span grid, which becomes denser near the supports and sparser directly under the light. When the light is off one sees only the solid surface underneath and when the light is turned on, the perforation pattern of the top surface shines through the variable density grid revealing the varying material densities inside. The surface itself is roughly normal to the major principal stress direction.

Local and Global Analysis

Oliver Bruckermann

**The REN building
for Shanghai
World Expo 2010**

BIG

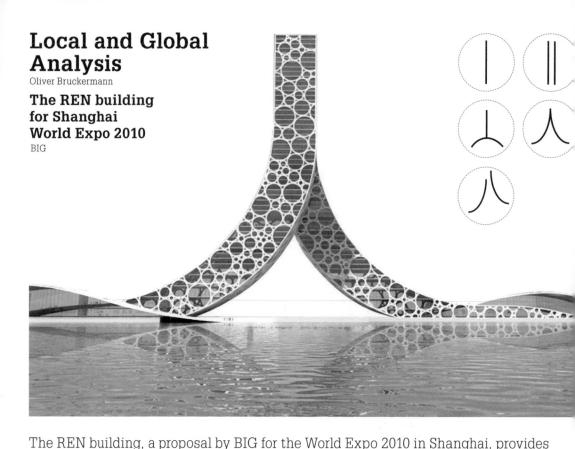

The REN building, a proposal by BIG for the World Expo 2010 in Shanghai, provides a fascinating basis for a parametric structural study of the interaction between global geometry and local structural elements within a new building typology. The building typology itself comes close to nirvana for a structural engineer by combining two of the most structurally pure forms, namely the bridge and the tower.

The building raises many structural challenges and tends to lead the design team along the path of employing the building facade as a primary structural stability element hence forcing detailed consideration of the interaction between the global building geometry and the details of local element to element geometry.

Our first step in carrying out the structural design on projects requiring collaboration between architect and engineer is to enter into face to face discussion with the architect and from this develop one or more structural concepts for the scheme to be advanced in more detail. On the one hand face to face discussions permit the engineers to gain an understanding of the architectural intent and to identify the architectural design priorities. On the other hand it allows the architects to benefit from an intuitive input from the engineers hopefully gaining an improved understanding of the dominant structural aspects of the current architectural proposals aiding them in advancing the architectural proposals in a way that tends to converge with the structural and construction requirements.

Many projects will benefit from a number of iterations of this intuitive interaction between engineer and architect, however the value of using this approach after the very early design steps is limited on many of the projects that AKT are asked to participate in due to the multifaceted combination of complex geometry and the strong interaction between architectural and structural forms. Such projects quickly take the structural concept beyond that which yields to rules of thumb and the structural engineer is no longer able to rely on past precedent to move the design forward, rather they must move into the arena of full structural analysis at an early design stage. The REN building falls into this category where engineering intuition has limited scope, but to some extent careful use of technology comes to the rescue.

The proliferation of ever more powerful structural analysis software opens up the opportunity for the engineer to embark on structural analysis of complete building models much earlier in the design process than was once viable. Advanced graphical user interfaces and in-house custom software interfaces work in tandem with improved analysis engines to make detailed structural analyses viable despite being in a situation where the architectural geometry of the project is still in a state of some fluidity. With this in mind one approach to responding to the challenge of creating a viable and economic structural solution for the REN building would be to carry out a structural analysis of the whole external primary support structure and to utilise this model to gain a detailed understanding of the overall structural behaviour as well as the structural properties required of individual structural elements. This analysis would provide an improved understanding of the behaviour of the structural form and acts as a firm foundation for the engineer and architect to work from in order to modify the structural and architectural approaches. Once likely modifications have been agreed these can be tested with further structural analysis, the extent and type of the proposed changes dictating whether a new full analysis is required or whether the analysis of localised parts of the model is sufficient.

When following this design methodology it is expected that a significant number of iterations around the analysis and geometry modification loop would be required before convergence between architectural and structural design requirements is achieved. Of course during the design process there will be many other constraints that must be incorporated, such as brief changes, building physics, budget constraints, etc., and these will tend to add constraints and complications slowing progress towards a convergent design.

Here we describe a proposal for investigating an alternative design methodology which employs a parameterised decision making model that can be used by both the architectural and engineering practices to drive the design forward in a controlled manner. Control is brought to bear by constraining the geometrical freedom of the architectural form using a set of bounded parameters, these parameters being chosen in such a way that structural viability of the form remains as the geometry is modified. The REN building is particularly appropriate for this approach due to the structural interplay between the proposed global and local geometries.

The principal considerations with respect to global geometry include:
- The overall building height.
- The length of the overall horizontal bridging span of the building.
- The offset distance between the two bridging legs of the building.

The principal considerations with respect to local geometry include:
- The maximum and minimum diameter of circle elements to be used in the structural façade.
- The maximum arc length between intersections of circle elements in the façade.
- The interaction of the floor plates with the façade

Some of the techniques that can be employed in defining the parametric rules in relation to the local geometry are discussed below.

The structural behaviour of a traditonal tower a is governed by axial compressive forces due to its self-weight, bending is induced by wind loads and seismic action. In a tower-bridge hybrid b bending moments in the sloping parts of the building result from the self-weight alone. To carry these moments and to limit deflections, the two legs of the building need to be very strong and stiff, respectively. In addition, the offset of the two legs of the actual design of the REN-building c leads to a twisting effect.

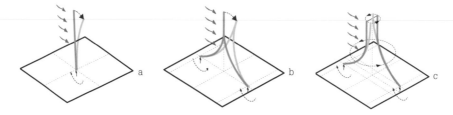

The influence of the offset has been analysed using a parametric model of the building with constant section properties. The rotation of the upper part of the building grows almost linearly with increasing offset. Despite the fact that the offset has a minor influence on the major axis bending moment the work done by the torsional moments in the legs of the building leads to increased vertical displacements.

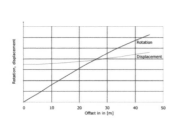

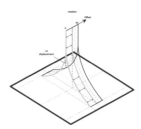

The dimensions of the zoomed "box" are relatively small compared to the overall dimensions of the building. Therefore, in the stage of conceptual design, it is sufficient to work out and design the properties such as axial and shear stiffness and torsional rigidity of such a box-section and use these values in the initial models.

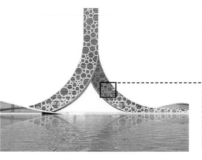

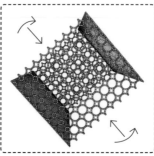

The mechanical behaviour of the box is governed mainly by the type of **circle-packing**. Rather than the randomised architectural proposal, here we analyse the behaviour of three more basic packings. Packing (a) is a regular grid of circles, packing (b) we use a staggered arrangement and with packing (c) a regular grid is extended by smaller circles as infills.

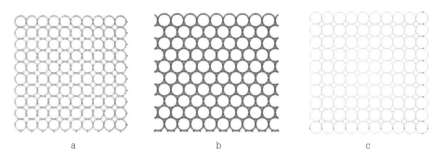

a b c

The **main characteristic influencing the stiffness of circle-packings** is whether bending or compression is predominant. The regular grid behaves similar to an ordinary (orthotropic) material. When it is vertically compressed it expands laterally. A denser mesh reduces this effect, ie the notional Poisson-ratio decreases. The main deformation of the unrestrained quarter-circles is due to bending rather than compression. Thereby the circles transform to ellipsoids. This option of circle-packing exhibits a rather soft behaviour.

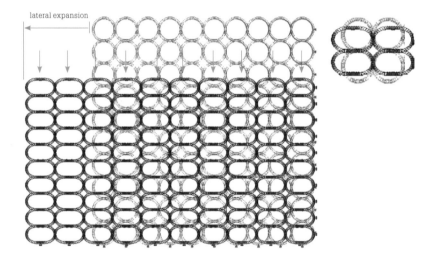

lateral expansion

Stiff compressive behaviour can be achieved by using smaller circles, ie a denser packing, or by an intelligent packing which reduces the angles between the intersections of the circles. The diagram shows qualitatively the stiffness of a pin ended arc element under compression as a function of the radius R and the angle j.

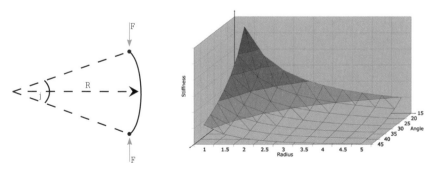

In the staggered circle-packing the angle j is always 60° whereas the option with small circle infills is characterised by 45° angles. In the graphs the compressive stiffnesses of the three options are compared. Using the same quantity of material, options b and c exhibit a much higher stiffness than the regular grid a.

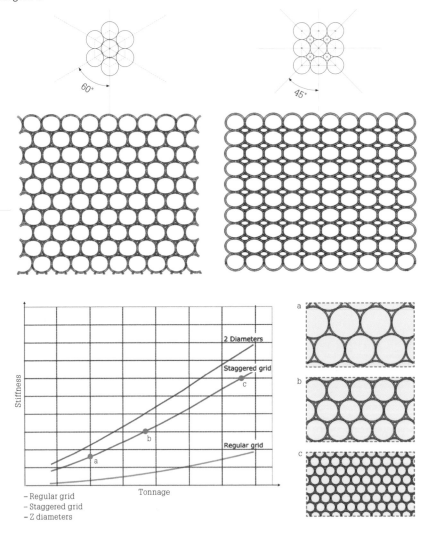

Based on the knowledge gained from a systematic parametric study it is possible to define a set of rules that allow the architect to generate complex circle packing arrangements which suit both the architectural and localised structural requirements for specific regions of the building facade.

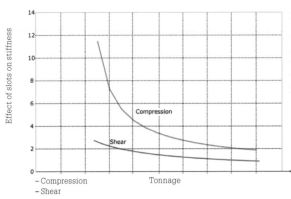

In the real structure the floor slabs are connected to the circle packed facade. The tensile stiffness of the slabs or edge beams can be utilized to restrain the lateral expansion of the circles, thereby reducing the notional poissons ratio of the façade structure.

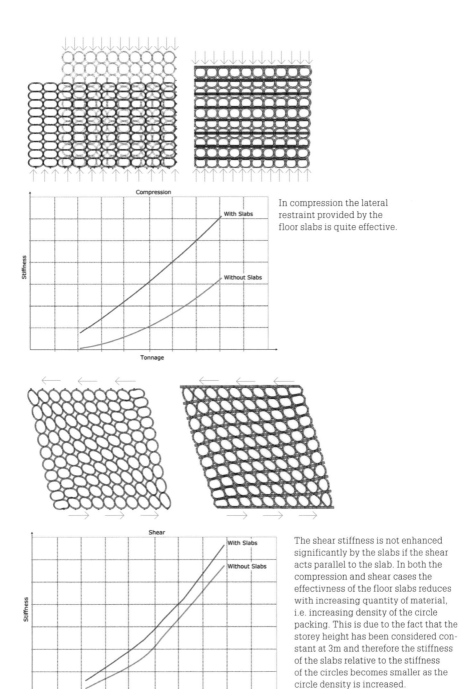

Compression

In compression the lateral restraint provided by the floor slabs is quite effective.

Shear

The shear stiffness is not enhanced significantly by the slabs if the shear acts parallel to the slab. In both the compression and shear cases the effectivness of the floor slabs reduces with increasing quantity of material, i.e. increasing density of the circle packing. This is due to the fact that the storey height has been considered constant at 3m and therefore the stiffness of the slabs relative to the stiffness of the circles becomes smaller as the circle density is increased.

The complete parametric rule set covers the whole building defining structurally acceptable limits for different interrelated aspects of the global and local geometry.

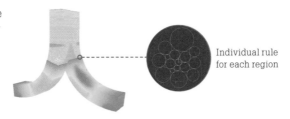

Individual rule for each region

Digital efficiency vs. physical necessity

The optimum, motivated by factors ranging from aesthetics, structures, and economics to environmental considerations, has a tight grip on the way we designers design today. Parametric tools enable a process where they facilitate design and collaboration between architects and engineers, allowing for the occurrence of research and ultimately the practice of design optimality. As members of p.art (parametric applied research team), our interest lies in questioning the development of this process of 'optimisation within parametrics' specific to materiality and fabrication. As we look at design processes we also examine and consider our currency[1], the parametric tool. Parametric tools in AKT currently help us to address various fabrication issues common to the industry. It is common that in such a commercial field materials are often chosen based on fixed design criteria relating to component sizes, thicknesses, opacities, and standard manufacturing processes. Naturally the ambition for the resulting built objects is a limited physical representation of a design that is generally crafted in the digital realm. In academia and contemporary practice the tool offers an alternative possibility to the above. The potentials it allows designers to digitally generate are immense. The sharing of data between models has also been made more seamless and efficient. But the glowing prospect of this type of computing power is not without controversy. New technologies widely available such as 3D prototyping, laser cutting and CNC enable for the rapid release of innovative designs, thus deferring the question of real physical and material allowances to later stages of projects. But why this is not questioned? Material considerations and parameters are of daily concern for structural engineers who in parallel to digital structural models still employ the use of physical testing. Tests such as these make it possible to reveal and anticipate unknown modes of structural and material behaviour that digital models are not able to anticipate and provide as they can only be constructed according to known patterns and parameters. Building and testing still remains as one of the truest ways of obtaining a 'real' sense of the physicality of structures. It cultivates an essential link between the two domains of abstract/ideal (digital) and real (physical and material). It is recognized that digital design has taken and maintained a stronghold on the movement of today's primary design processes, and it seems the interaction between digital efficiency and physical necessity is a companionship contemporary designers are at a pivotal point to interpret thoughtfully.[2] Modes of practice need to be redefined thoroughly and we as designers need to cultivate processes for intricate material crafting within the parametric realm. The utilization of techniques of examination and methods of evaluation from structural engineering, a discipline founded on the exploration and testing of matter is key for the introduction of consistent and precise material restrictions to 'parameterized' forms. These allow for the generation of mediums for creating approximations of geometry that act as mechanisms for controlling variations locally on materials, and allow for the measurement of performance. We are presently intrigued by a second digital revolution that will move past new methods of translation between software. One that goes beyond the realities of fabrication currently offered by the computer that merely allows designers to rationalize what has already been conceived.

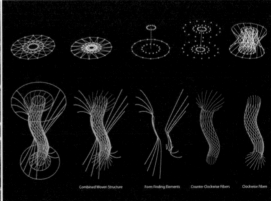

1, 2   'Bits and pieces' by Rebecca Roke (http://www.dhub.org/articles/157)

Workshop

Adiam Sertzu, Mei Chan

To date, Adams Kara Taylor has been inextricably involved with two significant workshops which are of interest to p.art for several reasons. It is essentially an arm of research explored physically and tested in real time. The setting forces architects, engineers and fabricators to open dialogues and to find a common design language that results in a hyper-laboratory-and-playground of undefined limit for experimentation and innovation. To date, AKT has been inextricably involved with two significant design workshops. Hanif Kara was invited to curate the International Concrete Competition'06 leading to the directing role of the Master class held in the Bauhaus, Dessau in September'06. We were again invited to act as a structural consultant jointly with the AA for the Fibrous Pavilion Workshop'07 held at ITU, Istanbul which is currently leading to the construction of a pioneering pavilion for the Istanbul capital of culture 2010. From the onset small teams comprising of both structural engineers and designers from p.art were configured and dedicated to engage with the workshops. By comparison, the two workshops had contrasting agendas. The Concrete Master class dealt with specific issues of materiality, kinematics and structure. On the other hand the Fibrous Workshop focused on parametric structures in conjunction with its physical counterpart.
As a research unit of architects that operate within an environment of engineers we re-address the parametric process, how possible it is to be able to embody material design and its behaviours. We commence our speculation from opposing ends; to explore parametrics in the context of materiality and conversely, to explore materiality within the context of parametrics. Drawing from findings of both workshops, a project was selected from each and developed in context to the questions posed.

esult of the workshops at Bauhaus in Dessau in September 2006 and at ITU in 2007 (the Fibrous Pavilion Workshop of AA).

Project 1: **Material to Parametric**

The concrete master class commenced from a purely material standpoint, the exploration of concrete in relation to the dual and combined qualities of the themes 'plasticity' and 'opacity'. While the projects were generally metaphorical, they allowed for the exploration of an engineering aesthetic in the solution. As the structural behaviours and tendencies of each project was examined in relation to the brief, the students simultaneously engaged with technical experts to experiment with and test various material possibilities. These findings were then translated to 1:1 scaled concrete models.

The student intuitively engaged with the plastic and opaque aspects of the brief using two simple materials; concrete and ice (then later plastic bubble wrap). The project was set out as a metaphor with the intention to abstract certain qualitative properties of the relationship between the two chosen materials which began at opposite poles of their metamorphosis states.

The grid circles on the bubble wrap were an interesting incident. When superimposed in layers and inadvertently placed and shifted in and out of registration or alignment, they formed light interference or cancellation patterns creating a moiré effect. Secondly this particular pattern with alternating honeycomb grid circles generated a specific type of (flower pattern) constellations. And finally, when a light source was introduced behind the patterns they grew to be intensely reflective. Evidently the field of moiré is wide ranging and requires extensive computational work. Thus, for the development purpose of this investigation, parametric tools are utilized only to explore this specific variation of moiré at a simple geometric level. It was a further object to look at the project in a manner that can be inexpensively manufactured using standard existing materials and standard manufacturing processes.

Fabrication sequence: The model is composed of four panels. The combination of two panels enables for the casting of a honeycomb like surface, allowing for the removal of formwork from both sides to be reused. The resulting double layers will be connected mechanically via connections cast into the concrete panels at specified points.

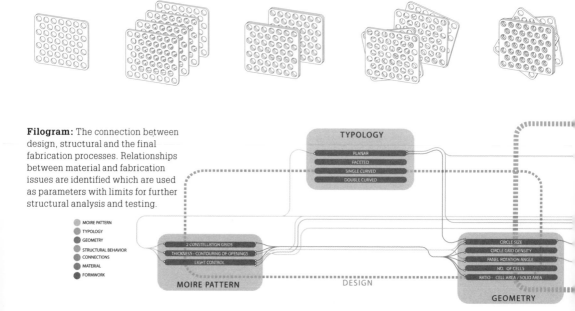

Filogram: The connection between design, structural and the final fabrication processes. Relationships between material and fabrication issues are identified which are used as parameters with limits for further structural analysis and testing.

- MOIRE PATTERN
- TYPOLOGY
- GEOMETRY
- STRUCTURAL BEHAVIOR
- CONNECTIONS
- MATERIAL
- FORMWORK

TYPOLOGY
PLANAR
FACETED
SINGLE CURVED
DOUBLE CURVED

MOIRE PATTERN
2 CONSTELLATION GRIDS
THICKNESS - CONTOURING OF OPENINGS
LIGHT CONTROL

DESIGN

GEOMETRY
CIRCLE SIZE
CIRCLE GRID DENSITY
PANEL ROTATION ANGLE
NO. OF CELLS
RATIO - CELL AREA / SOLID AREA

composite moiré panel composed of 4 patterns at varying angles. And the final result from the Bauhaus master class.

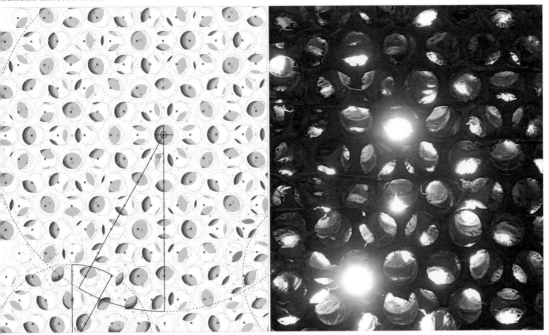

The project was tested to an extreme, projecting it at a scale that is 5m x 5m and 30mm thick. Initially concrete with a minimum panel thickness was explored. Once fixed, panels with various moiré patterns and opening distributions were analysed to compare stresses and deflections, they were then assessed for use on particular locations of the 5m x 5m wall. The removal of formwork and transportation which would add extensive forces on to the panel were also considered. The type of concrete chosen for the purpose of this investigation was high strength fibre reinforced concrete which can withstand stresses of $250n/mm^2$ in compression and up to $30n/mm^2$ in tension. The benefits of this specific concrete type is that it eliminates the need for steel reinforcement bars, its fluidity can be controlled to deal with complex geometries and it achieves high early age strength which is ideal for fragile pre-cast concrete elements.

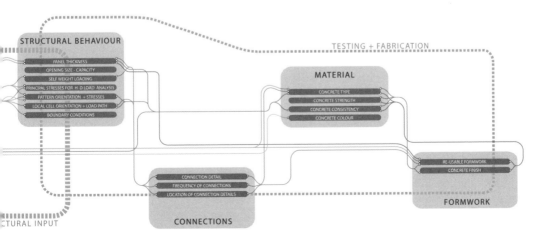

Project 2: **Parametric to Material**

The Fibrous workshop in Istanbul focused on structures comprised of fibrous elements generated by the means of parametric digital design via pre-identified organisational systems of bundling, weaving and branching. The primary material for the physical exploration was concrete. The workshop was structured to sub-divide members of each group to be dedicated to either the digital parametric design or physical material design, executing their research concurrently.

The weaving project was prime for further speculation. The physical model was a structural failure because the aggregated material system was too weak on a large scale. The pre-dominant factor that contributed to its failure was the fabrication process. The fabrication techniques were far too complicated, as it involved weaving the rope around extensive formwork by hand which proved too time consuming and inaccurate. The projects positions itself as the second iteration, bringing together the digital and physical exploration into one process. It springs from determining fixed design criteria, the fabrication process needs to be re-addressed to make it realisable. It was decided that the cast concrete fibre was the more appropriate method of construction.

What we had learnt from the other projects was that 3 dimensional fibres were extremely difficult to produce accurately, therefore the fibre would be broken down into parts which were able to be manufactured by casting it flat. This would mean that the components would be in effect, 2 dimensional fibres. The main concern with this constraint would be that the 3 dimensionality of the design would be compromised. The next design criteria is that the fibre would be as slender as possible. We learnt from the workshop that 50 mm needs to be the minimum diameter for it to be structurally viable. Taking these 2 additional design rules and existing logics of the group's organisational model, a parametric model was re-built.

The muquarnas was the starting point of the project.

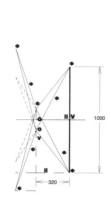

Geometrical logics were abstracted, providing the basis for the parametric model.

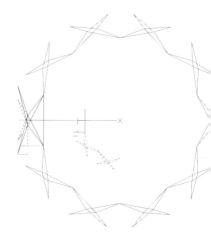

Each weaving template consists of 10 tiles arrayed radially.

he next layer of information would be structural constraints. A single layer of weave
as structurally inefficient therefore the new organisational model had incorporated a
ouble layered weave. The points of connection are another factor that was considered.
he analyses of the weaving structure in turn was able to inform changes to the
arametric weaving template that would be structurally advantageous.
he ambition for this speculation is that with the material input into the parametric
nodel, the design would be structurally successful and also be able to retain some
f the qualitative features we discovered the physical models to have embodied.

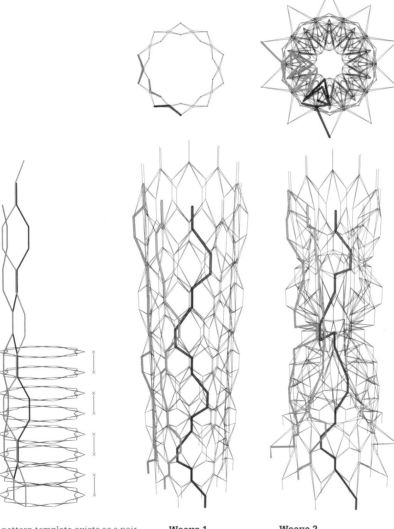

The 2 methods of casting concrete into the tubes.

The first method is to prepare the model formwork as a whole to have only one concrete pouring session. The advantages of this method is that it reduces the need for assembly later on. However, the preparation of the form-work becomes complicated and difficult to control result-ing in low accuracy.

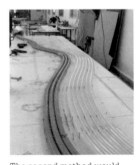

The second method would be to prepare the fibres as components to be assembled when the concrete is set. The tubes are filled with concrete and then put into its form-work. Casting the tubes as 2 dimensional elements affords a greater degree of accuracy and commands formwork that is less convoluted.

h pattern template exists as a pair
design fabrication parameter. This
ld create fibres which can be broken
n into 2 dimensional components
t can be easily made and assembled.

Weave 1
Default weaving
schedule.

Weave 2
Parameters can be adjusted
according to design and
structural input to craft the
overall weaving form.

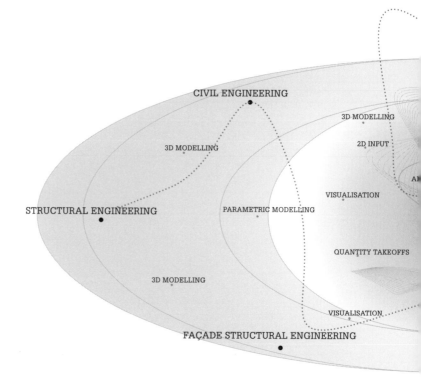

CIVIL ENGINEERING

3D MODELLING

2D INPUT

3D MODELLING

VISUALISATION

STRUCTURAL ENGINEERING

PARAMETRIC MODELLING

QUANTITY TAKEOFFS

3D MODELLING

VISUALISATION

FAÇADE STRUCTURAL ENGINEERING

Analysis modelling
Investigating the digital material
p.art

As has been exemplified in the previous articles, the AKT identity is intimately linked with the way in which the engineers of AKT interact with the specialist competence of p.art. This enables AKT to continuously develop the way by which the link between geometric organisation principle and structural behaviour is defined; hereby strengthening the bond between the daring thought and the equally challenging constructed. The concept of p.art capitalises on the idea that structural engineering intuition assist architectural freedom of thought. The efforts of p.art are therefore concerned with setting up robust work routines for studying the relation between form and performance. For this purpose p.art recognises that the contemporary digital toolkits of the two disciplines are complimentary, and that the successful synthesis of parametric and structural analysis modelling results in an empirical design environment for the investigation of innovative formal vocabularies.

The two modelling platforms at the technical core of p.art are employed as parallel, iterative methods for describing active geometric relations—resulting in the creation of synchronised, flexible data networks with the capacity to reconfigure in a coherent manner. A parametric model may in this context be described as a strategy for modelling 'fluid geometric states', the main feature of the model being its immense capacity for detailed description and control of geometric dependencies and hierarchies for setting up the latent rules underlying manifest form. Once these interdependencies are created, the system is open to endless adjustments, changes 'rippling' through the system according to the way by which the various constituent parts are

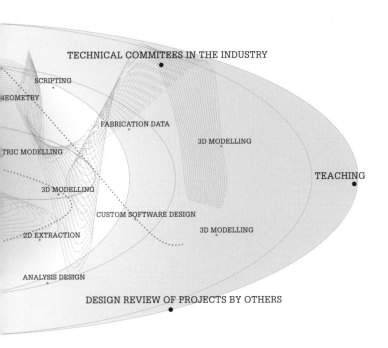

TECHNICAL COMMITEES IN THE INDUSTRY

SCRIPTING

GEOMETRY

FABRICATION DATA

3D MODELLING

TRIC MODELLING

TEACHING

3D MODELLING

CUSTOM SOFTWARE DESIGN

3D MODELLING

2D EXTRACTION

ANALYSIS DESIGN

DESIGN REVIEW OF PROJECTS BY OTHERS

et up to affect, or be affected by others. This may be compared with the informa-
on depth of the structural analysis model, where the latent rules created according
o the experience of the structural engineer become evident as the simulation runs.
n the case of the parametric model, there is however no 'system driver' equal to the
oading scenario in the structural analysis model, and also no actual means to dif-
erentiate between various 'states' of the system. Introducing structural analysis as a
omplimentary evaluation method at an early stage in the design development process
ctivates the immense capacity of the parametric model; maximising the benefit of a
model type that is simultaneously rigorously defined and in constant flux. On the other
and, structural analysis modelling is essentially rooted in existing typologies, since
 is built up around qualified assumptions and the application of existing typologies.
troducing parametric modelling as a parallel strategy unlocks the innovative poten-
al of the structural engineering study, since it allows the engineer to 'step out of'
is/hers past experiences, and to instead playfully explore various structural solutions
n response to a design proposal. Achieving a synergy of parametric and structural
nalysis modelling throughout the various architecture scales enables an in-depth
tudy encompassing material tolerances, structural typologies, manufacturing ratio-
ales, shape grammars, etc. In this manner, AKT is able to 'activate' the potency of a
roposed design concept, through the thorough investigation and development of its
material-structural properties and resultant capacity. The cross-disciplinary profile of
.art firmly positions the firm in the creative mid-ground between the architectural
phemeral and the engineering pragmatic, with the possibility to reach beyond estab-
shed systems and traditions.

designtoproduction

brings together the practical experience of Arnold Walz a
"geometry consultant" and the academic research of the
former *caad.designtoproduction* team founded by Fabian
Scheurer, Christoph Schindler and Markus Braach at Prof
Ludger Hovestadt's Chair of CAAD at ETH Zürich. design
toproduction implements digital process chains based on
parametric CAD-models and offers consulting services
for parametric planning, detailing, optimization, and digital
manufacturing. **www.designtoproduction.com**

The Whole and its Parts

All architectural structures—unless dug into the earth—have this one thing in common: they are assemblies of numerous parts joined together. This statement is based upon the simple fact that no single material, be it natural or manufactured, is as large as a building. In architecture, the whole easily consists of thousands of parts. And if the architect used contemporary digital-modeling tools to generate complex form, each element of the design is probably different.

In today's building process it seems that the introduction of digital design and fabrication tools leads to a continuous flow of information from conception into production. In the architect's practice, computer-aided design (CAD) software helps to define surfaces by pulling control points or adding and subtracting volumes like a virtual sculptor. Via standard data formats the design is forwarded to computer-aided manufacturing (CAM) software in the workshop, which in turn controls the computerized tools that produce the various components. Does 'CAD/CAM' mean that architectural design is reduced to pulling control points, exporting the result and leaning back to watch the production?

This method indeed is applicable to small-scale prototype design or mold fabrication where the whole consists of just one part. In architecture however, the whole and its parts are not identical: CAD modeling-tools help to define the whole, while a CNC-machine fabricates parts. And even worse, the building material at disposal within the budget often does not match the desired shape: plain sheets and straight bars and profiles confront curvilinear designs.

How to translate the shape of the whole into parts made from standardized material? Here in fact, between the modeling tool and the fabrication tool, lies the complete architectural planning process including the breakdown into parts, the optimization according to various constraints, the detailing, and the preparation for fabrication. There is neither a generic software tool to automate this process from the whole to its parts. Building designs are too different for a generally applicable solution. Nor is the manual processing of thousands of different parts advisable, because it is laborious and hard to get a grip on it. Approaching a digital architectural planning process means establishing project-specific algorithmic relations between the whole and its parts.

designtoproduction researches and realizes automated solutions for the intermediate steps between digital design and digital fabrication. Those steps are interconnected: they influence each other from the whole to the parts and from the parts to the whole until the information and material flow is harmonized.

We identify four different steps between architectural design and machine driver:

1. ORGANIZE the relation between the whole and its parts:
Parametric 3D-CAD models

To organize dynamically the breakdown from the whole to the parts, we implement customized parametric models on the basis of professional CAD packages.

Complex systems are spatially difficult to comprehend. The intertwining forms of UNStudio's Mercedes-Benz Museum for instance can hardly be described in plans and sections. However, contractors needed exact documents with information about the parts while the whole was still in the process of development.

By organizing the immense amount of information in a parametric three-dimensional model a couple of thousand detailed plans could be generated automatically for any variant of the design chosen by the architect.

Designers don't think in numbers. They think in relations. Standard CAD systems don't store relations. They store numbers. Numbers that change while their relations remain stable. Parametric CAD models capture those persistent rules behind the developing form, reducing thousands of coordinates to a handful of parameters.

The consequence of describing thousands of different parts with a few parameters is a new kind of 'parametric standardization': Individuality is expressed in variables.

2. OPTIMIZE the whole depending on the interrelations among its parts:
Algorithmic optimization tools

designtoproduction identifies relations among the parts to develop advanced optimization tools that match design ideas to the best constructive, structural, and functional solution.

The leaning columns in the basement of KCAP's Groningen Stadsbalkon have to hold up a 3000 sqm concrete slab, get out of the way, minimize resources, and give the impression of a random forest. Such conflicting demands are hard to tackle with a systematic approach. With an optimization software based on artificial-life methods the architects were enabled to "grow" alternative solutions on their screens that matched all constraints—far quicker than a real forest.

In a rectangular design with regular grids and uniform modules the optimum is easy to determine. But in a complex geometry, where dimensions change and angles vary, it can be difficult to find any answer at all—let alone a good one. With state-of-the-art optimization tools that exploit the power of bottom-up methods like Genetic Algorithms and Swarm Intelligence it is possible to find good solutions for complex systems—maintaining the non-regular form instead of falling back on a square grid.

3. SIMPLIFY the parts:
Rationalizing the parts to realize the design

Architectural construction is all about the assembly of parts.
And complex architecture consists of large numbers of individual parts.
One of our favorite details is a little extruded aluminum dovetail profile that we used for several constructions. While the little profile is a standard invariable industrial product, the grooved counterpart on the component is a parametric detail. More than three thousand of them are needed to connect the 2164 pieces of Daniel Libeskind's sculpture Futuropolis. And besides looking good each of them saved a few minutes of labor time, because they make it unnecessary to clamp the pieces during the hardening of the glue.

Integrating thorough knowledge about fabrication technologies, materials and joints into the detailing leads to smarter, leaner, and more rational production processes—and to a result that comes close to the intention of the original design without busting the budget. We attempt to produce detailing strategies that reflect a deep understanding of the methods and constraints of existing fabrication processes. In fact, most of the conditions for breaking down the whole into parts are determined by machines' dimensions, its tools and scope of movement. We seek for constructive solutions to cover systematically the range of individual, parametric details.

4. MATERIALIZE information:
Production data for the parts

Non-standard geometries are built from non-standard parts. In a workshop, every single part has to be edited for the computer-aided machine—nesting parts in raw material, selecting tools, configuring the tool path and generating the machine code.

The doubly curved glass panels on Zaha Hadid's Hungerburg Funicular Stations are held in place by some 2500 individually shaped profiles. Each of them is cut from polyethylene boards with a computer controlled five-axis router. Manually nesting a couple of thousand pieces and translating their geometry into NC-programs for the router would have been a heavy burden for any building budget. Therefore, the complete machine code was directly generated from a parametric 3D-model —including stickers with unique part-IDs that help allocate the pieces.

While software solutions offer to perform many of those steps automatically, still every single part has to be imported and treated with CAM software tools —an enduring process that has to be repeated any time a condition changes. Automating the planning from detailing to machine code is the final step of organizing the relations between the whole and its parts, but is adding most value to the processing chain.

Zentrum Paul Klee

Renzo Piano, Bern 2004

A series of gradually diminishing "waves" on a concentric grid forms the roof structure of the Zentrum Paul Klee in Berne/Switzerland. In addition to their changing curvature and size, some of the roof beams also incline at different angles, resulting in a geometry with quite complex interdependencies.
To accompany and support the design process, a parametric model was developed. It enabled the architects to test countless alternative solutions until the final design was determined. And in a final step, it was used to generate the construction documents for the steel contractor.

Here, the development of the whole and its parts was achieved by an integrated process in three steps:

2. 3D parametric waves: The three-dimensional geometries of the waves are built on the grid. From the result, any kind of section and view can be derived to check the geometry during the design phase.

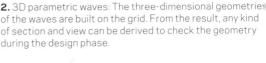

1. 2D parametric grid: The design concept is translated into a two dimensional parametric grid, which determines the positions of the ridges and valleys of the roof.

3. Deduction of steel geometries: The geometry of the curv I-beams is mapped to two-dimensional plans for the contrac tor, including webs and flanges. Also the geometry for the sheet metal cladding of the I-beams and the roof is unfolded

Architect → **Renzo Piano Building Workshop (RPBW), Paris: Morten Busk-Peterson** Site management → **ARB Arbeits-gruppe, Bern** Geometry consulting → **Arnold Walz** Structural engineering → **Ove Arup International Ldt, London**

Peek&Cloppenburg Weltstadthaus
Renzo Piano, Cologne 2005

The façade of the P&C department store Weltstadthaus in Cologne posed quite some challenges to design and engineering. The most difficult one being the ubiquitous question of how to tile a doubly curved surface with planar glass panels – how to break down the whole into reasonable parts.

For budget and constructive reasons, the panels had to be flat and quadrangular, which resulted in an offset between the corners of each four panels meeting in one point. Also, the panel-sizes had to change continuously in order to give the overall impression of a smooth surface. To solve both problems, a parametric façade model was developed by designtoproduction partner Arnold Walz.

This made it possible to iteratively optimize the horizontal and vertical panel segmentation until the maximum deflection for all 6500 glass panels reached values less than 6mm—a tolerance that could be absorbed by the window sealing.

For every intermediate step, a complete 3D model of the façade construction and detailed plans and sections could be generated automatically—in the end providing the final documentation for the façade contractor. Also, a direct export to an engineering software allowed for structural integrity testing.

Architecture → **Renzo Piano Building Workshop, Paris (Project manager: Eric Volz)** Client → **Peek & Cloppenburg KG, Düsseldorf** Geometry consulting → **Arnold Walz** General contractor → **Hochtief AG, Essen** Structural engineering → **Knippers Helbig, Stuttgart** Façade → **Schmidlin AG, Aesch**

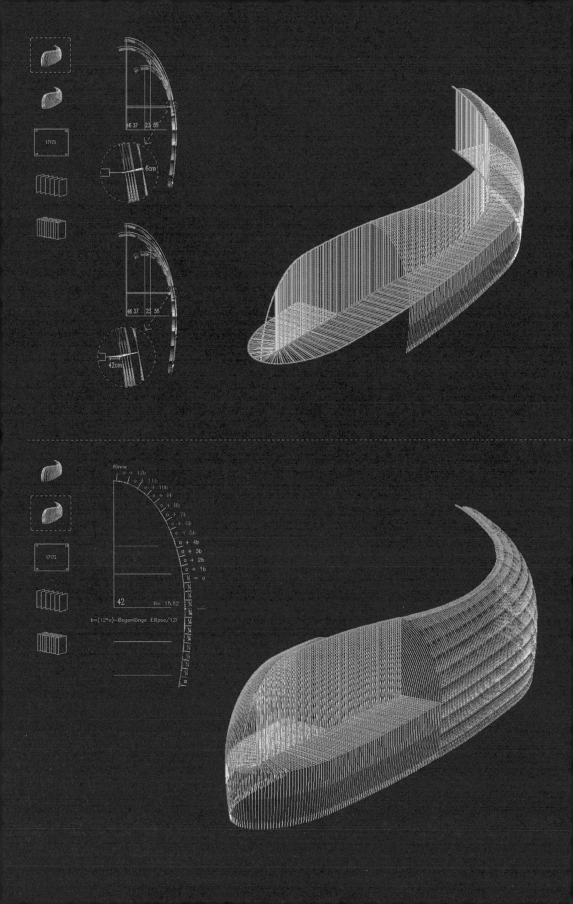

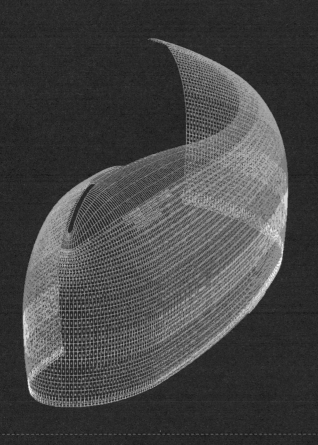

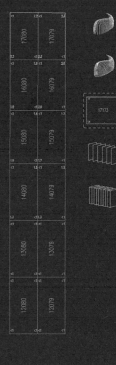

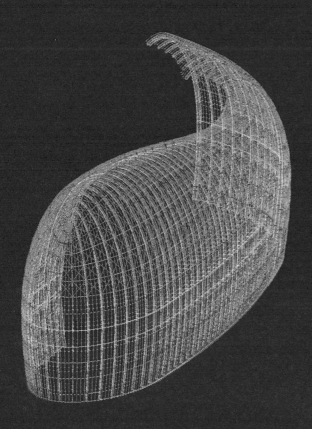

Mercedes-Benz Museum

UNStudio, Stuttgart 2005

he parametric model for the Mercedes Benz Museum not only described
part of the building, like the façade or the roof, it was the universal key to the con-
truction: the model formed the foundation for the construction documentation of
ll doubly curved parts and linked the participating trades in the building to
harmonic whole. Basically everything in this extraordinary design was coordi-
ated and decided with the help of the parametric model, be it the dimensions of
he cores, the width of the ramps, the dimensions of the concrete slabs, or the ceil-
ng heights. The whole design was developed from a two-dimensional composition
f circles, tangents, and intersection points, gradually reduced to the geometry
ecessary to describe the design.

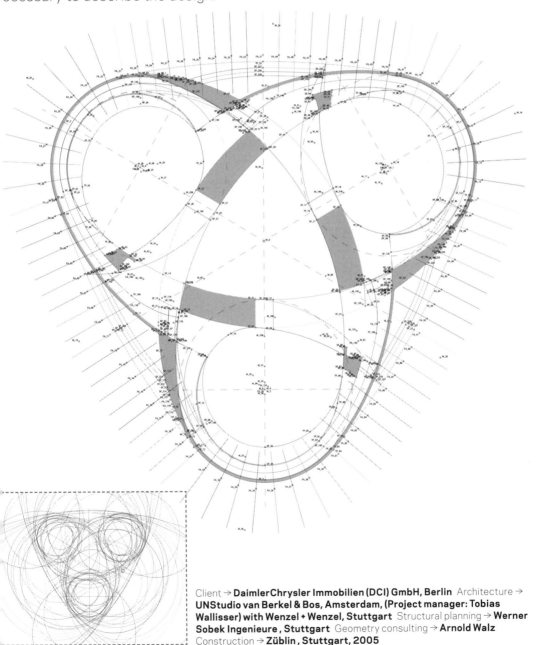

Client → **DaimlerChrysler Immobilien (DCI) GmbH, Berlin** Architecture →
**UNStudio van Berkel & Bos, Amsterdam, (Project manager: Tobias
Wallisser) with Wenzel + Wenzel, Stuttgart** Structural planning → **Werner
Sobek Ingenieure , Stuttgart** Geometry consulting → **Arnold Walz**
Construction → **Züblin , Stuttgart, 2005**

From this basic geometry, the edges of the three-dimensional concrete volumes were generated by transforming the planar curves into constantly rising spatial curves. This parametric master model contained all geometric data for the process of planning and building: horizontal and vertical sections, point coordinates of all rising curves, façade and beam geometries, the development of curved sections as well as the data for digital production.

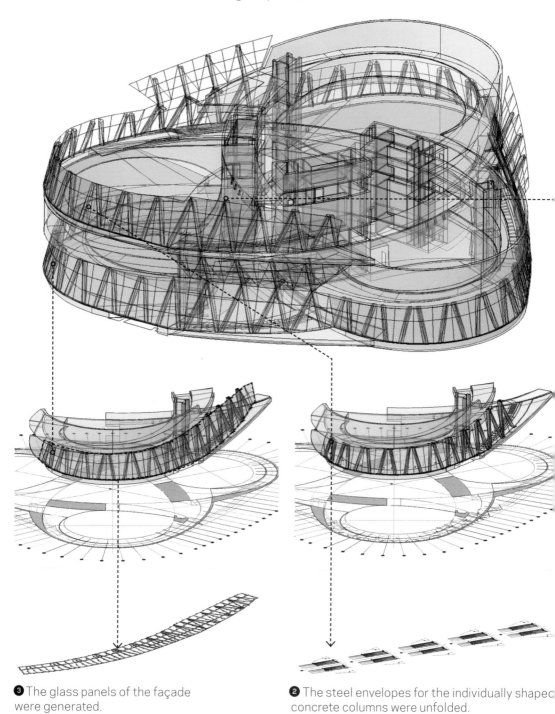

❸ The glass panels of the façade were generated.

❷ The steel envelopes for the individually shaped concrete columns were unfolded.

or three different building components the constructive geometry was directly
erived from the model, thus closing the chain of information from early design
tages until the construction and fabrication phase. → ❶ ❷ ❸

The formwork for the doubly curved
oncrete surfaces was accurately
eveloped into plain boards that could
e bent to the desired shape during the
onstruction process.

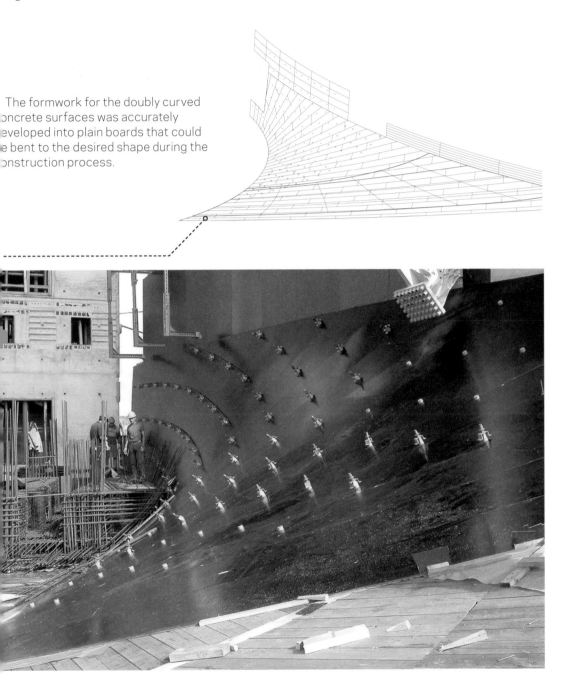

© Wout

The Groningen Stadsbalkon illustrates a design approach where the whole is organizing itself in a bottom-up process based on the interrelation of its parts.

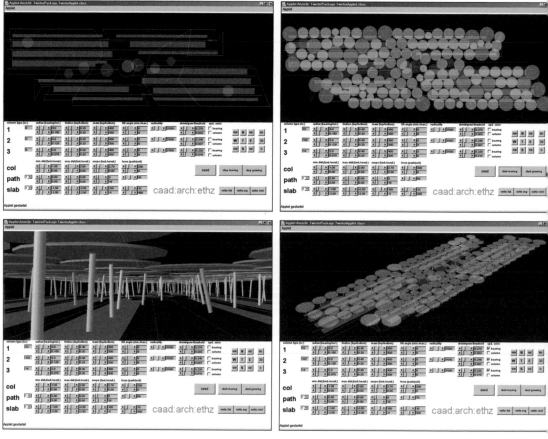

caad:arch:ethz

Geometry consulting → **ETH Zurich, caad.designtoproduction: Fabian Scheurer** Architecture → **Kees Christiaanse Architects & Planners KCAP, Rotterdam: Andy Woodcock** Engineering → **Ove Arup + Partner, Amsterdam: Arjan Habraken** Site → **Groningen, 2003**

Groningen Stadsbalkon
Kees Christiaanse Architects & Planners, Groningen 2003

Building a forest of columns For the new Stadsbalkon (balcony of the city) at central station Groningen, Kees Christiaanse Architects and Planners (KCAP) proposed a semi-underground bicycle garage with a pedestrian area on top, supported by some 150 inclined pillars that were randomly dispersed in the basement—a "forest of columns".

The challenge was to define the exact location, diameter and inclination of every single column so that it would ensure the stability of the structure and not obstruct the predefined walking or cycling paths. Also, the total number of columns and their strengths had to be optimized. Simple rules provided by the structural engineers related the column diameter to the optimum distances between columns and the edge of the slab, but since every local change in one column would influence its neighbors and therefore propagate through the whole structure, it was virtually impossible to optimize the whole configuration in a top-down approach.

Every column is an agent According to the concept of agent-based systems, a software simulation was programmed where every column is an independent agent that locally interacts with its neighbor columns (by pushing them if they come too close) and with the environment (by trying to keep the right distance to the slab's edges and staying away from the paths). In addition, to optimize the number of columns, the agent population is able to grow and shrink. If a column senses no direct neighbors it starts to increase its diameter and thus the desirable distance to its neighbors. When it reaches a defined maximum value it may split into two columns of the smallest size, increasing the number of columns in the habitat. Reversely, when the pushing from different directions gets too hard, it reduces its diameter and eventually removes itself from the habitat.

The architects could interactively influence this bottom-up process by changing various control parameters as well as by directly dragging selected columns to desired spots whereupon the rest of the whole immediately tried to rearrange, always ensuring that the system stayed within the structural and functional prerequisites. The simulation model proved to be very successful and enabled the architects to develop a number of possible solutions within a few hours. The best-performing alternative was selected for realization.

Swissbau Pavilion
ETH Zürich, Basel 2005

   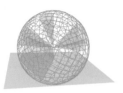

he Swissbau Pavilion is the first project where designtoproduction integrated
ll the steps between the whole and its parts, between design and fabrication,
nto one continuous chain of digital information processing. The pavilion was
esigned and built to exhibit the latest results of CAAD research at ETH Zurich
uring the Swissbau 2005 building fair in Basel. It has the form of a sphere with
our meters diameter and is assembled from 320 wooden frames, each consisting
f four wooden boards standing perpendicular on the surface of the sphere.
While in a traditional coffered dome a regular structure dictates the placement
f openings, here the frames are required to adapt their size and angles to the
eliberately asymmetric placement of windows.

imulating a growing mesh To generate this adaptive geometry, a custom-built software simulates
he growth of a quadrilateral mesh on a sphere following simple rules: the edges try to align with the
ositions of the predefined openings and the floor level, while at the same time every frame attempts
o optimize its size and angles in regard to constructive constraints. Under certain circumstances
he structure can locally alter its topology by inserting or deleting frames until it reaches
 stable state. The simulation is running in real-time and the user can directly influence the structure
y displacing nodes on the sphere.

utomated machine code generation For production, the generated geometry is imported into
 parametric CAD model, which generates the exact geometries of all 320 wooden frames and their
280 parts, including the connection details. All parts are automatically numbered, laid out flat
nd nested on the OSB boards used for milling. The G-Code for controlling a CNC-router that is fabri-
ating the parts is generated for every board. It already includes information for drilling the holes and
illing the unique part-ID into the boards.

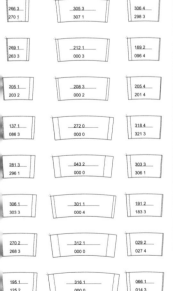

Organization → **I-Catcher GmbH, Basel: Ruedi Tobler, Felix Knobel** Geometry
consulting and engineering → **ETH Zurich, caad.designtoproduction:
Christoph Schindler, Fabian Scheurer, Markus Braach** CNC-production →
Bach Heiden AG: Franz Roman Bach, Hansueli Dumelin

© Jürg Gasser

175

Inventioneering Architecture

Instant Architects, Travelling Exhibition 2005

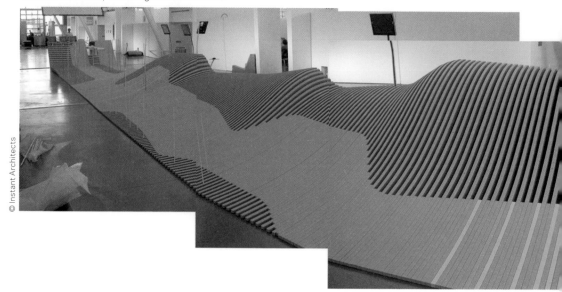

© Instant Architects

In the Inventioneering Architecture project, the whole and its parts influence each other: while the whole explicitly determines the geometry of all parts, the production method chosen for the parts is prominent in the appearance of the whole. The project is a traveling exhibition of the four Swiss architecture schools (Zurich, Lausanne, Geneva and Mendrisio) that was shown in San Francisco, Boston, Berlin, Dubai, Shanghai, Tokyo and Singapore. This doubly curved platform resembles an abstract crosscut through Swiss topography. It measures 40 by 3 meters with varying heights up to 1.5 meters. A footpath meanders along the surface, passing the exhibits.

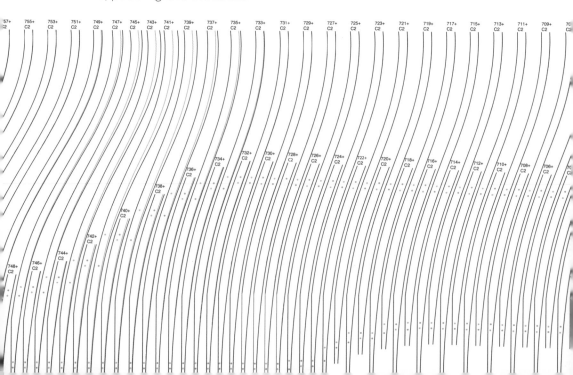

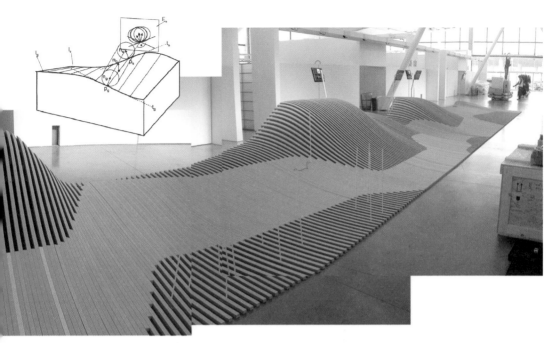

,000 individually curved rafters designtoproduction proposed to assemble he platform from 1000 individually curved rafters that were milled out of medium ensity fiberboard (MDF). They are assembled in comb-shape, so that their verlapping sections form the closed surface of the path while the exhibition area s marked by gaps. By choosing a rather cheap material and implementing a contin-ous digital chain from the definition of the surface geometry in the CAD software Maya until the control of the five-axis CNC-mill that the parts are manufactured vith, production costs could be lowered significantly.

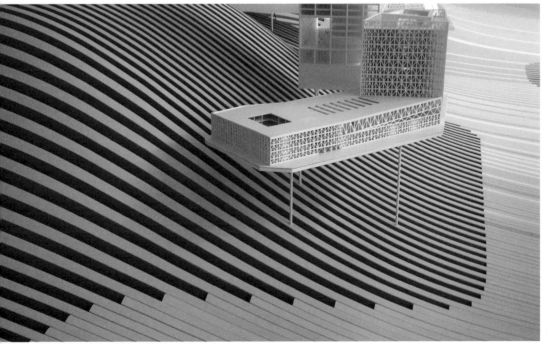

The twisted cut: a doubly-curved surface with a single movement
The detailing was developed closely after the capabilities of a five-axis router.
The platform is divided into 40mm wide cross sections, each describing the upper
surface of one rafter. To produce this surface, the milling tool follows both edges
and rotates around its path, cutting a "ruled surface" that follows the topography of
the platform both along and across the section. Thus it is possible to manufacture
a three-dimensional, doubly curved surface from two-dimensional sheet material
at very low cost. The rafters are connected by dowels and supported by perpendicular boards.

Automated detailing and production planning Since the structure consists
of more than 1000 individually shaped parts, the crucial point was to automate
the translation of the platform geometry into the part geometry and finally into
the machine code controlling the CNC router. This was accomplished by a set of
scripts on a standard CAD system. The first script imports the original design
defined as a NURBS-surface in the modeling software Maya, reads the coordinates of the platform's cross-sections for every rafter and determines the angles
of bank. A second script translates this information into the milling paths for all
rafters, also including the drillings for the dowels. A third script arranges and
optimizes the rafters on the MDF-boards and generates the G-Code programs,
which control the movements of the five-axis CNC-router.

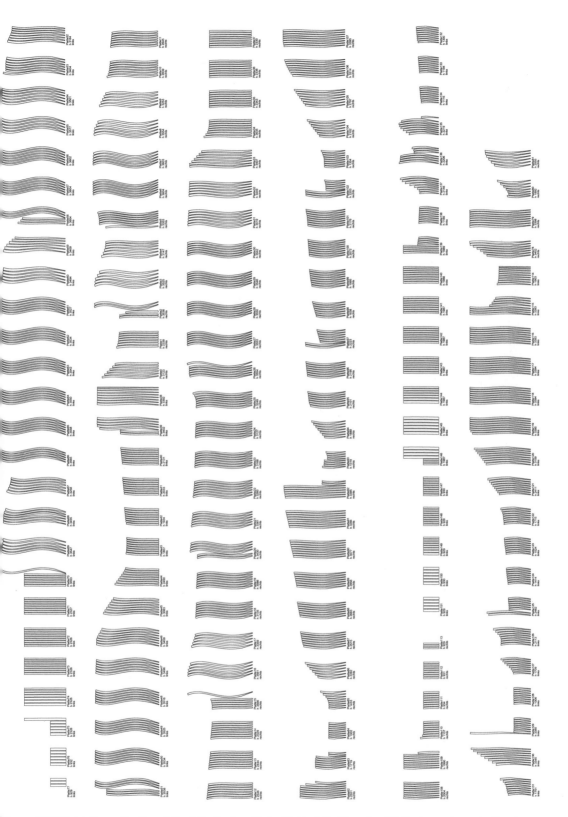

Client → **ETH Zürich Executive Board: Prof. Dr. Gerhard Schmitt, Prof. Dr. Marc Angélil** Design and organization →
nstant Architects, Zürich/Berlin: **Dirk Hebel, Jörg Stollmann** Geometry consulting and engineering → **ETH Zürich,**
aad.designtoproduction: **Christoph Schindler, Markus Braach, Fabian Scheurer** CNC-production → **Bach Heiden AG:**
ranz Roman Bach, Hansueli Dumelin

HUNGERBURG FUNICULAR
Zaha Hadid, Innsbruck 2007

The Hungerburg project directly uses the fabrication methods developed for Inventioneering Architecture, showing the transferability of experience from one project to another. Only this time the work of designtoproduction had to be seamlessly integrated into a large scale construction and fabrication project. For the four new stations of the Hungerburg funicular designed by Zaha Hadid in Innsbruck more than 2000 meters of custom cut polyethylene (PE) profiles connect the glass cladding of the roof to the steel ribs of the support structure. Since the roof surface is a doubly curved free-form, the profiles constantly change their angle of bank while following the ribs. Again, the "twisted" five-axis-cut, already tested on the Inventioneering Architecture project, was applied. The geometry of the profiles was provided by the engineering partner in the form of spline-curves in a CAD-model. designtoproduction automated the segmentation of the profiles, the placement of drillings, the nesting on boards, and the generation of G-Code for the 5-axis CNC-router fabricating the parts. Also all production documentation, including part lists and stickers with the unique part ID and information for subsequent production steps of every part, were generated. Production was executed just in time for every station, following the pace of the construction process and enabling last-minute changes to the geometry. With more than 2500 individually shaped parts, the Hungerburg project resulted in the highest number of fabricated parts so far.

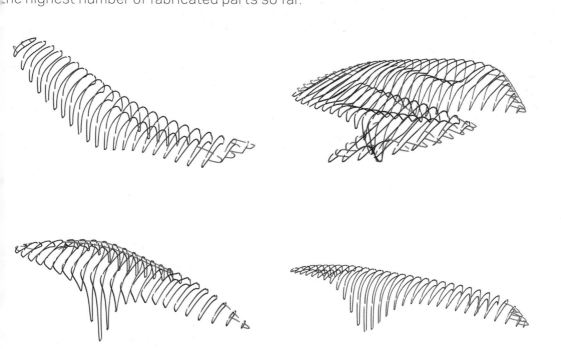

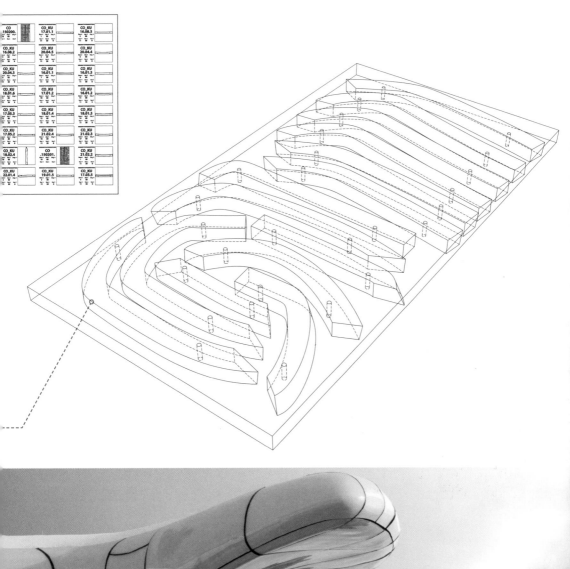

Architecture → **Zaha Hadid Architects, London**
Engineering → **Bollinger Grohmann Schneider
Zivilingenieure, Vienna: Arne Hofmann** Fabrication
planning → **designtoproduction: Fabian Scheurer**
CNC-production → **Bach Heiden AG, Heiden:
Hansueli Dumelin**

Libeskind's Futuropolis
Daniel Libeskind, St. Gallen 2005

Futuropolis, the whole and its parts are algorithmically defined by the intersec-on of two sets of extruded profiles. Everything from appearance to detail in this ghly complex structure can be traced back to this geometrical operation. uturopolis is a wooden sculpture designed by Studio Daniel Libeskind for a work-hop held at the University of St. Gallen (HSG) in October 2005. The design is ased on a triangular grid, where a 98 tightly packed towers form an ascending vol-ne of up to 3.8 meters height. The structure results from an intersection of two milar sets of extruded profiles based on a grid of equilateral triangles, that cut ach other in an angle of 25 degrees. The client had searched in vain for six month l over the world for somebody who dared to build this structure in the given time nd budget frame.

implifying with a dovetail-connector

ne first challenge was to find an appropriate construction method to materialize iis geometric idea. We proposed a structure of wooden boards. In order to guar-ntee maximum structural integrity at minimum production and assembly costs, ie detail for connecting the different parts was crucial for the whole project. y using aluminum dovetail-connectors and cutting the necessary miters and otches with a CNC-router, it was possible to reduce the number of connection ariants to only ten different types and completely automate the fabrication of ie connection detail.

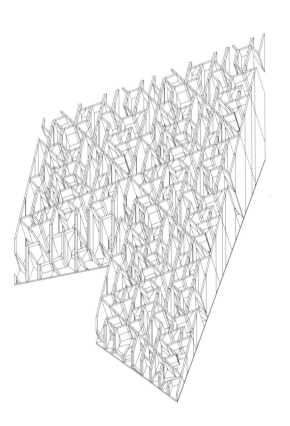
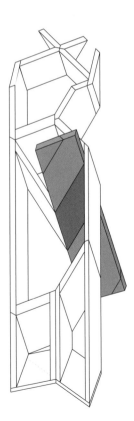

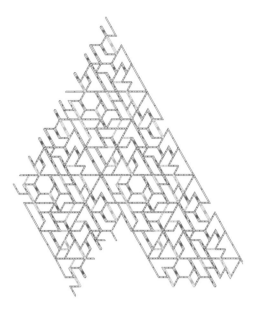

Organizing 2164 different elements

The second challenge was to generate the exact geometry of all 2164 parts resulting from the intersection, including the bases of the towers. A completely parametric CAD-model of the sculpture was developed, which calculated the outline of all parts by closely following the algorithmic design rules given by the architect. The appropriate connection details where automatically assigned to the edges, the parts were numbered and arranged on boards.

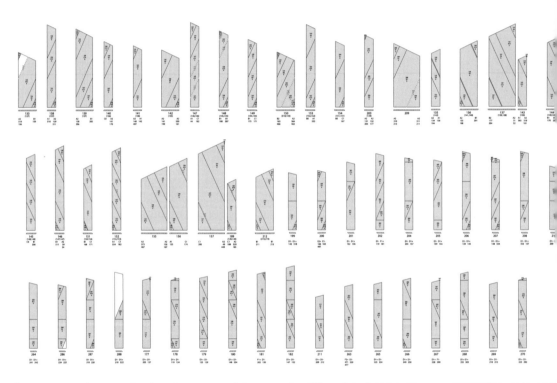

Automated translation into machine code

The third step was to translate this geometry information into the machine code for the CNC-router. Since the boards had to be turned around in the middle of the production process, two G-Code programs per board had to be generated by a script. Also the exact widths and lengths for calculating the material costs and for preparing the raw boards were automatically exported as spreadsheets. The sculpture consists of 360 square meters of 32 mm thick boards, altogether almost 11.5 cubic meters of birch wood.

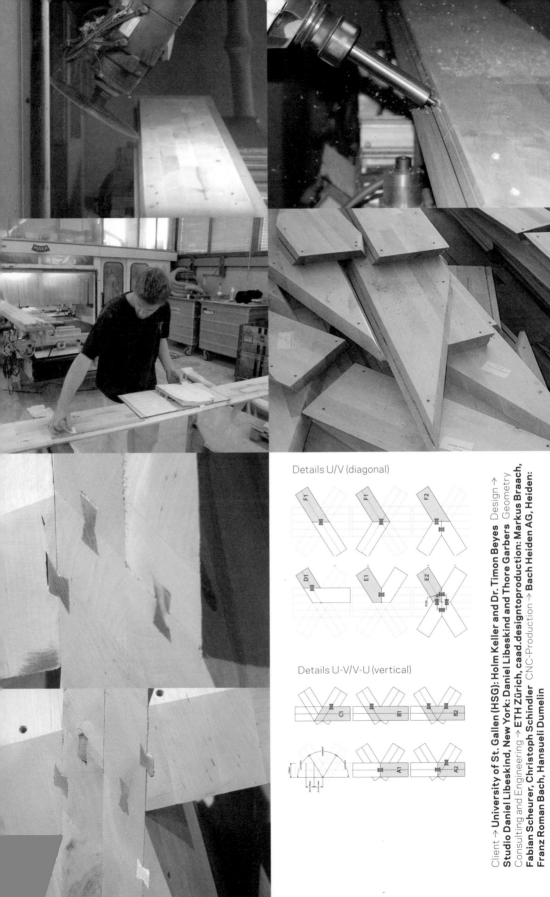

Details U/V (diagonal)

Details U-V/V-U (vertical)

Client → University of St. Gallen (HSG): Holm Keller and Dr. Timon Beyes Design →
Studio Daniel Libeskind, New York: Daniel Libeskind and Thore Garbers Geometry
Consulting and Engineering → ETH Zürich, caad.designtoproduction: Markus Braach,
Fabian Scheurer, Christoph Schindler CNC-Production → Bach Heiden AG, Heiden:
Franz Roman Bach, Hansueli Dumelin

ZipShape
Research project 2007

The manufacturing of curved parts in timber construction is very laborious for small series, prototypes and individual production. To define the curvature during the forming and joining process, special molds are needed, representing a high time and cost factor for small series. This holds true for the processing of plywood, as well as for slotted bendable panels from materials such as wood, composite wood products and gypsum plaster boards.

Bending without mold ZipShape introduces a method that makes it possible to manufacture single curved panels from any plain material without molds or jigs. This patented system uses two individually slotted panels that interlock when bent to a defined curvature. That way the curvature is already precisely defined through the joining process. With individually shaped teeth, any developable surface can be described unambiguously. Additional elements, that are not part of the final product, are not needed. The analogy between this joining process and a zip induced the name of the method.

Automated planning process The geometry of the teeth is depending on the geometry of the desired curve. A manual planning method (CAD-drawing, hand drawing) is inadequate because of the geometrical complexity of the joint, the resulting error-rate and the drawing effort. Likewise, it is hardly imaginable to craft such a toothed panel with the necessary precision by hand in an appropriate time-frame. Therefore, an automated planning process (processing information) is linked with a machine tool (processing material).

Two individually slotted panels interlock when bent to a defined curvature.
That way the curvature is already precisely defined through the joining process.

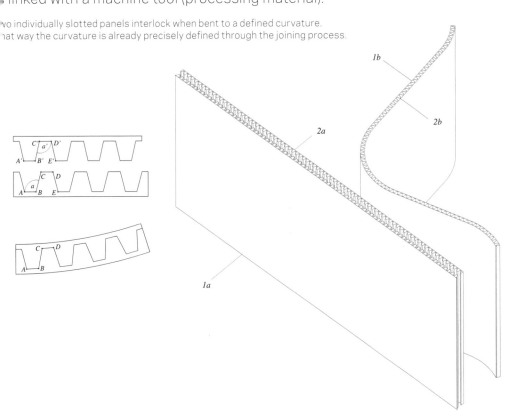

The ZipShape-method is a promising alternative to existing methods, especially for small series (interiors, prototypes) and larger curved elements. Thanks to the automated detailing the complex interlocking is not cost-relevant. While many applications of CAD/CAM are solutions for specific complex design ideas, this method aims to be a general approach to realize curved shapes in an economical and attractive way and illustrates how ordinary building processes can be advanced with integration of information technology.

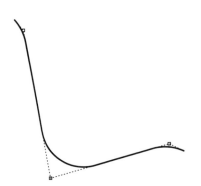

1 Manual curve definition with a common CAD-software

2 Automated detailing: From the curve geometry, the shape of every individual slot in the two boards is generated In the process, the following parameters are variable: material thickness, tooth width, tooth height, tooth inclination. The related script was realized in Vectorscript, the scripting language of Nemetschek Vectorworks.

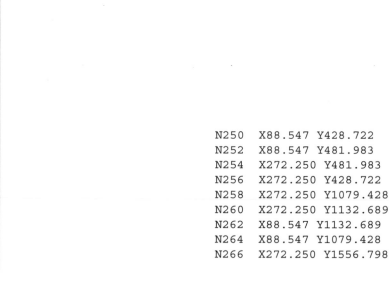

```
N250   X88.547 Y428.722
N252   X88.547 Y481.983
N254   X272.250 Y481.983
N256   X272.250 Y428.722
N258   X272.250 Y1079.428
N260   X272.250 Y1132.689
N262   X88.547 Y1132.689
N264   X88.547 Y1079.428
N266   X272.250 Y1556.798
```

3 Automated unfolding: The detailed elements are unfolded to be manufactured from plain panels.

4 G-code generation: From the unfolded geometries, the G-Code (machine code) is deduced automatically.

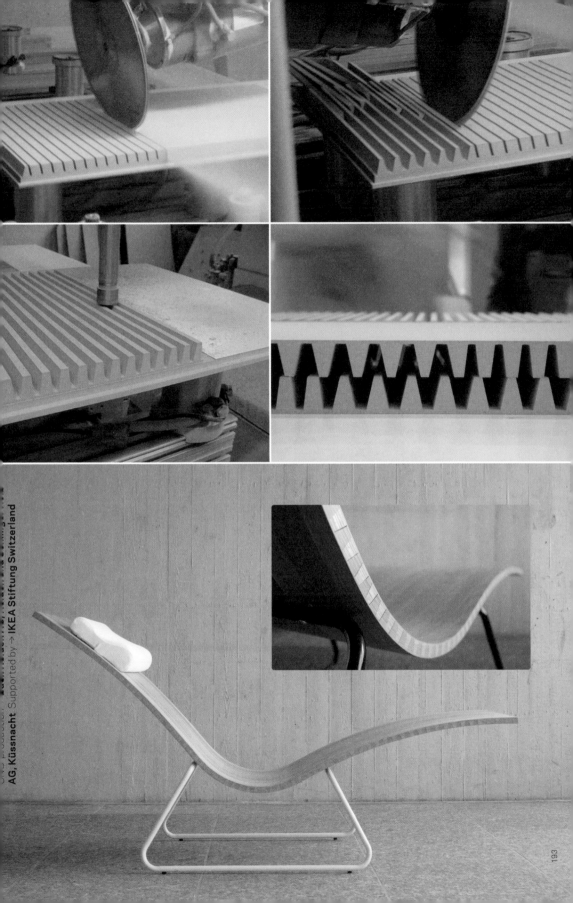

AG, Küssnacht Supported by → IKEA Stiftung Switzerland

Aranda/Lasch

is a New York-based architectural studio founded by Benjamin Aranda and Christopher Lasch in 2003 after graduating from Columbia University. The think of their practice as a way of putting together craft and computation through geometry, mathematics and pattern. Their research on physical pr cesses and biological systems is illustrated in the Brooklyn Pigeon Project (an investigation of pigeon swarms) and the Pamphlet Architecture public tion *Tooling*. **www.terraswarm.com**

Baskets
2006

What is parametric to us?

We once built some baskets with a Native-American basket weaver named Terrol Johnson, and learned we have much in common. Before Terrol, we had always described our approach to design as *computational*, since we preferred to create our own design tools rather than purchase them. This meant we could use a very fundamental type of language, computer code, to build up our concepts, whatever these may have been. Our exchanges with Terrol taught us something else: that with any technique—whether one calls it craft or computation—there exists a certain disengagement from the object being formed; the process becomes more about the *relations* around that object.

Terrol spoke of basket-making as a process that brings people together, both those around him and the ancestors through which he continues a tradition. He spoke of many voices in that object, as if each basket was, in essence, a conversation. So too, we began to think of making architecture as a conversation between themes of universal significance, such as geometry and matter, with the actual experiences through which these themes become manifest. It is a boundless and inspiring conversation, one that reminds us that designing can be about communing between two worlds: one entirely abstract and coded, the other very real and alive, like what we find through our interactions every day with people, communities, and cities. In the end, like those baskets, the truly inspired moment of design comes with the realization that neither of these worlds is of our own making—both were always there, and somehow discovered along the way.

Out of Order

Design: Aranda/Lasch (Benjamin Aranda, Chris Lasch) Commissioned by Paul Johnson of The Johnson Trading Gallery

Our obsession is the pursuit of orders that are rigorously modular but wild—almost out of order. *Quasicrystals*, a new phase of matter discovered in 1984, represent this kind of material structure that hovers on the edge of falling apart. They are like crystals in that they are solid, but they also display characteristics of completely disordered media, like a liquid. They are neither one nor the other. Unlike a regular crystal, whose molecular pattern is periodic (or repetitive in all directions), the distinctive quality of

a quasicrystal is that its structural pattern never repeats the same way twice. It is endless and uneven, but interestingly, it can be described by the arrangement of a small set of modular parts. *Modularity* has long been an animating impulse for architecture, but here it is offered with a twist: the possibility of having the efficiency of modularity without the stagnation of information that conventional repetition entails. This prospect has proved rewarding, albeit difficult and a bit scary, for our office.

Quasi Cabinet, 2007

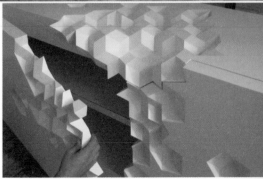

Monsters The key to quasicrystals' aperiodic structure is that they are organized by so-called "forbidden" symmetries (such as 5, 8, or 12-old symmetries) that, until recently, were not thought to be able to tile space without leaving gaps. The mathematician Johannas Kepler was one of the first to take up the challenge of tiling with these forbidden symmetries in his book *Harmonice Mundi* of 1619. When asked if he had succeeded in tiling the plane with 5-sided shapes, he ominously affirmed that he had, but found that there are "monsters" in the resulting order. In this case, the monsters were pairs of fused decagons, an unexpected shape. These kinds of order are more frightening and gory than those found in the wildest fiction, precisely because they appear despite our best attempts to remain rational and discrete.

In 1974, Roger Penrose decomposed Kepler's four tiles into a pair of two specially-shaped tiles that could only tile the plane aperiodically. In so doing, he proved mathematically once and for all that an aperiodic tiling could exist, at least in theory. Both had succeeded in producing a 5-sided tiling, but the Penrose pattern was periodic and always changing.

Aperiodic patterns can carry more information that repetitive ones. The *problem* is that this amount of information is overwhelming. The seemingly impossible combination of local stability paired with ultimate long-range unpredictibility accounts for the pattern's shift between form and formlessness. It is not that the pattern is unstructured, but that it threatens our conception of what order is, and our ability to control or even understand it.

Shadows In 1982, the material scientist Dan Schectman discovered a new type of solid-state matter. Like a regular crystal, it consisted of densely packed molecules, but unlike a regular crystal, its structural pattern displayed a remarkable character: it never, ever repeated the same way twice.

The kind of order exhibited by Mr. Schectman's sample was not unfamiliar, as aperiodic packings had been recently well described in theory. What was surprising, though, and is today still a mystery, is how such a thing could exist in reality.

How can molecules, which assemble themselves using only local forces, be found organized in complex examples of long-range order? In order to orient themselves correctly, each molecule would have to "know" what was happening in far-away parts of the pattern—and this is impossible.

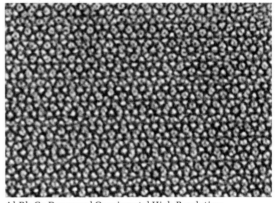

Al-Rh-Cu Decagonal Quasicrystal High-Resolution Electron Microscopy image showing the aperiodic arrangements of atoms.

Icosahedral Al6Li3Cu displaying triacontahedral faceting.

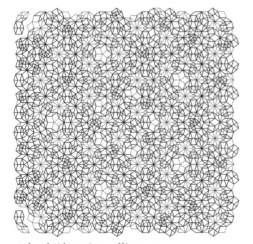

2-rhomboid quasicrystalline pattern

Quasicrystalline studies

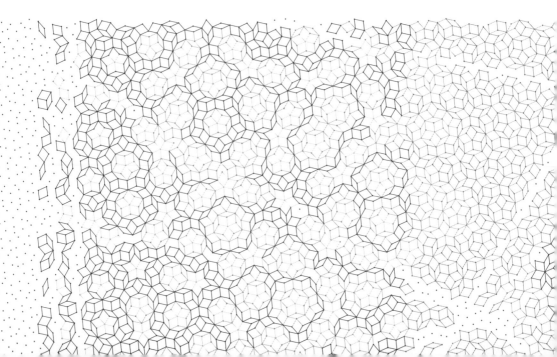

Projection In 1974, Roger Penrose had discovered his pattern through trial and error, identifying two tiles which, when put together in a certain way, would accomplish an aperiodic (non-repeating) covering of the plane. In 1980, Nicolaas de Bruijn created an algorithm that turned Penrose's intuitive tiling into a rule. His projection algorithm is a near-perfect description of quasicrystalline order; the only problem (and not just for architecture) is that it is an existential one. It explains quite reliably how a quasicrystal might form, but to do so, it resorts to using projection from a higher dimension down to our more familiar two or three-dimensional space. The implication, then, is that when we see a natural quasicrystal and hold it in our hands, what we are dealing with is actually a hyper-dimensional object—only its shadow exists here in our reality. How de Bruijn made the conceptual leap necessary to find the algorithm of projection from higher dimensions has never been fully explained, but his equation remains for us a bridge to another reality and back.

Quasi component mock-up

Quasi Table Plan

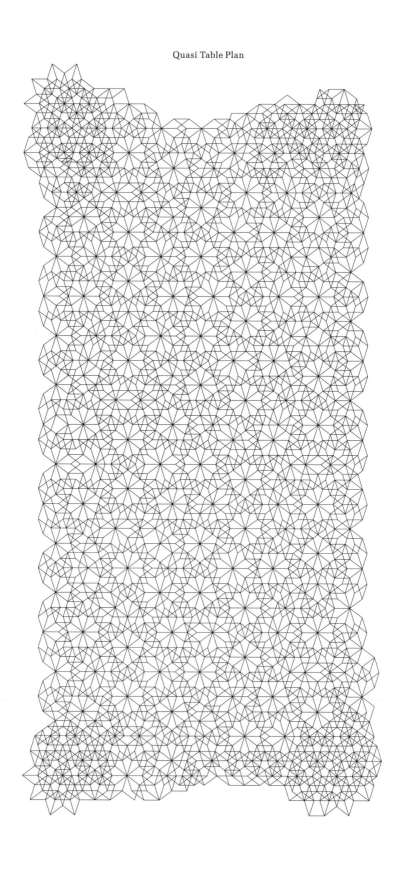

Difficulty So how does one make something out of a substance that is visiting from another dimension? For a series of furniture experiments we wondered what would happen when a higher-dimensionality occupies the mundane stuff of our daily lives, like a table or a cabinet. In these projects, the template of a common furniture element functions as a filter to look at the quasicrystalline packing, giving a unique vantage point to explore its odd grains and contours.

The Year 1774

Design: Aranda/Lasch (Benjamin Aranda, Chris Lasch, Clay Coffey) Commissioned by Paul Johnson of Johnson Trading Gallery

Two things happened in the year 1774. Louis XV, the "Beloved King"—by then reviled for his monarchy's excesses in the face of a looming insurgency—died, the sunset of one of history's most lavish monarchies. In the same year, a young Swede named Johann Gahn, working in the deepest and wettest levels of a mine, fired a crucible lined with a mixture of charcoal, oil, and ore to discover Manganese, a trace element critical for life processes in plants and animals. At a molecular level, when combined with oxides, the metal displays a striking "super-crystal" modularity. In the following experiments, this nexus of events—the super-excess of Louis XV and the super-crystal of Manganese—are fused into a single moment of design.

Louis XV by Hyacinthe Rigaud (1730)

Louis XV style armchair, The Fauteuil

1774 Series Fauteuil, 2007

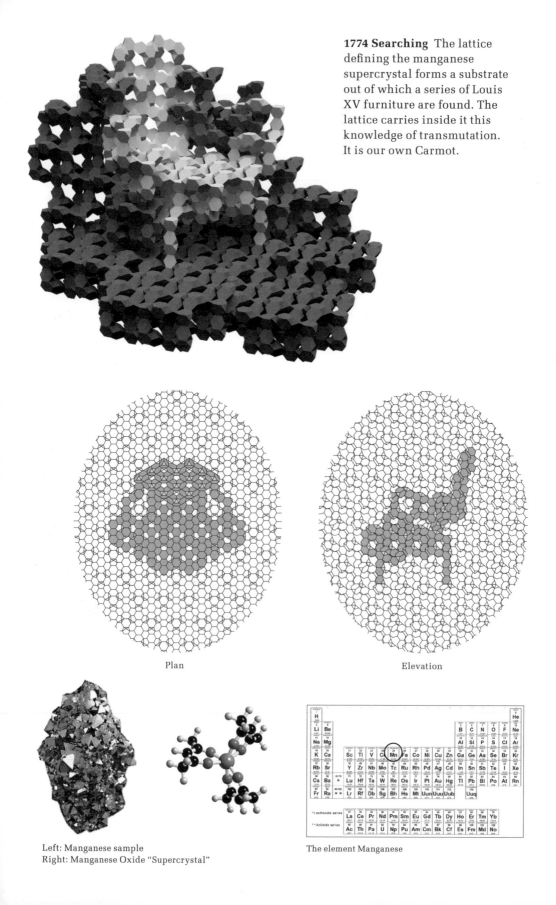

1774 Searching The lattice defining the manganese supercrystal forms a substrate out of which a series of Louis XV furniture are found. The lattice carries inside it this knowledge of transmutation. It is our own Carmot.

Plan

Elevation

Left: Manganese sample
Right: Manganese Oxide "Supercrystal"

The element Manganese

Cardboard Mock-up

Color Shift

Concept: Benjamin Aranda & Chris Lasch, terraswarm
Video director: Scott Kuzio
Video production: Carole McClintok
Digital assistant: Matthew Achterberg
Large format & digital photography: Stefan Hagen
FreshDirect: Neal Bayless, Philip Emeott, Jim Moore
Curator & instigator: Mark Wasiuta
Installation: Andrew Ballard
Special thanks to: Anh Tuan Pham
Colorshift was exhibited at Columbia University's school
of architecture in 2007. The exhibition was produced with
generous support from the owners of the LED billboard,
FreshDirect, and Columbia's Graduate School of Architecture,
Planning and Preservation.

The presence of media in the city is difficult to ignore. Often this persistence of lights, images, words and sounds is associated with advertising. Worse, it is sometimes described as pollution, disordered and confusing. When looked at through the lens of networked technology, however, this is just one side of the spectrum. Embedded in all media is the potential for orchestration, rhythm, and harmony. Large-scale media can be recognized as a dynamic, a field of output available for control. Color Shift is a project that enters this dynamic of big media, twists it, and renders it at a very large scale. Color is one way to get inside, to project order and behold its effect on the city.

Big Sign FreshDirect is an online grocer changing the structure of food buying and distribution in New York City. Orders are placed on their website and then delivered to doorsteps within twenty-four hours. FreshDirect inverts the traditional relationship between physical space and marketing to great success: replacing the usual grocery store's aisles and check-out lines are fleets of refrigerated trucks; instead of the usual storefront stands an animated billboard that dwarfs anything in Times Square.

Greeting incoming traffic about to enter the Midtown Tunnel is the FreshDirect billboard, the largest outdoor video billboard in the country. Towering 165 feet above ground and measuring 90 feet wide by 65 feet tall, the FreshDirect sign operates seven days a week, 24 hours a day and reaches an estimated 35 million people annually.

While intended for drivers along the Long Island Expressway, the sign's scale and effect can also be appreciated for miles around New York, especially at night. In addition to delivering advertisements, the FreshDirect billboard establishes a mood for the neighborhood by illuminating entire sections of Long Island City with its flickering glow.

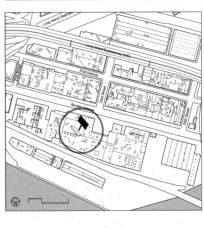

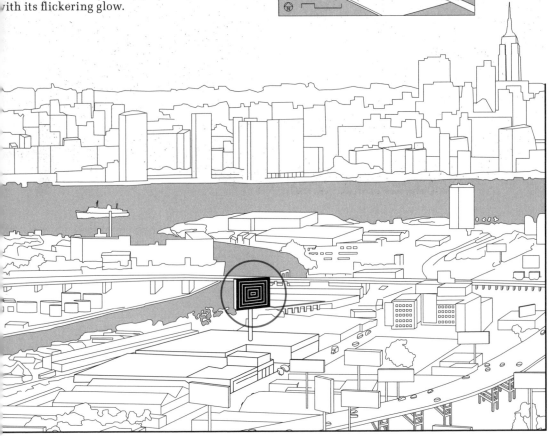

The LED billboard is made up of a large array of LED blocks (shown above), each of which contains 3072 pixels. Standard video input can be converted to billboard-ready artwork using a scaler/converter.

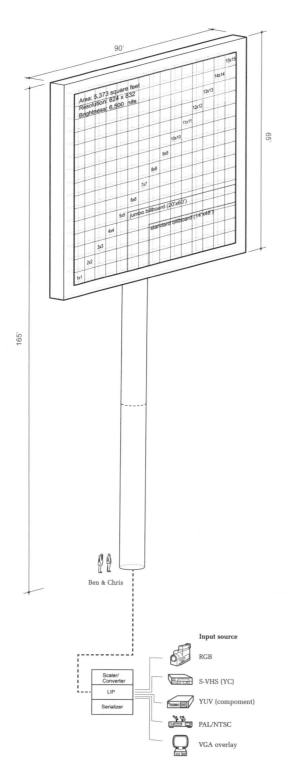

90'

15x15
14x14
13x13
12x12
11x11
10x10
9x9
8x8
7x7
6x6
5x5   jumbo billboard (20'x60')
standard billboard (14'x48')
4x4
3x3
2x2
1x1

Area: 5,373 square feet
Resolution: 624 x 832
Brightness: 6,500 nits

65'

165'

Ben & Chris

Input source

RGB

S-VHS (YC)

YUV (compoment)

PAL/NTSC

VGA overlay

Scaler/
Converter
LIP
Serializer

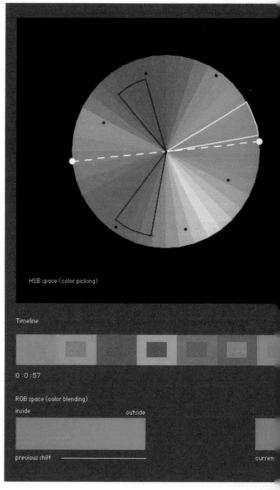

HSB space (color picking)

Timeline

0 : 0 : 57

RGB space (color blending)

inside   outside

previous shift ——————————   curren

RGB space

Enter the dynamic of RGB space. A sequence of color fields replaced the giant billboard's regular advertising on a series of evening in the months of February and March of 2007. The color fields were generated by an algorithm using the open-source software, Processing. The way the colors shift is like a "dance" around the color wheel. Specifically, a mixture of analogous colors appears for 30 seconds before transitioning 150 degrees around the wheel to another mixture of complimentary colors, resting for 30 seconds and moving around yet again. This dancing was designed to push two aspects of color shifting. First, it produces the maximum color value from the LEDs, i.e. the greenest of greens, the reddest of reds, etc. Second, it pushes the perception of color depth by oscillating between analogous and complimentary colors.

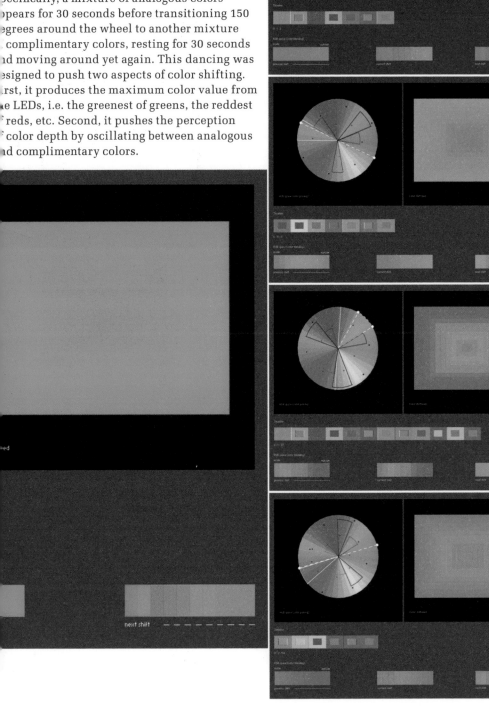

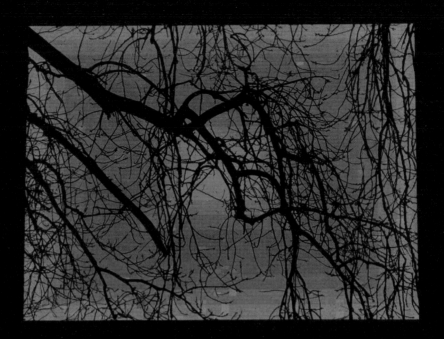

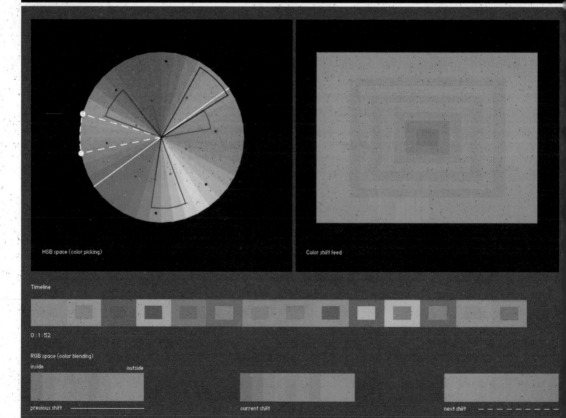

HSB space (color picking)

Color shift feed

Timeline

0 : 1 : 52

RGB space (color blending)

inside   outside

previous shift _____   current shift   next shift _ _ _ _

Pysche

When we approached the company with a plan to replace their billboard's advertising feed at night with a series of colors and then record its effects, we were surprised at how receptive they were to the idea. They liked that other people appreciated their billboard's scale because, as we came to learn, the billboard had become part of their company's psyche. We were able to buy media time at a fraction of its actual cost—a convergence of marketing and media with contemporary urban and art practices.

The capacity of tools to create new things, lies in their ability to guide our understanding in between things. Synthesis is ultimately more interesting, more powerful. As the tools we fashion become less about what they are and more about the relationships they create, their expression in our work becomes less and less distinct until, as in Color Shift, they entirely dissolve into atmosphere. New organizations are created not to study them from the outside, but to inhabit them from within.

Sanford Kwinter

Sanford Kwinter is a writer, editor and philosopher with a background in comparative literature. Co-founder of Zone Books with Jonathan Crary and Bruce Mau, he was involved in the ANY series of conferences and has published among other *Pandemonium: The Rise of Predatory Locales in the Post-war World, Mutations, Architectures of Time: Towards a Theory of the Event in Modernist Culture* or his recent *Far from Equilibrium*. He is currently a visiting associate professor at the Harvard University Graduate School of Design and the head of Studio !KASAM, a content and communications design firm.

Jason Payne

Jason Payne is co-founder (with Heather Roberge) of the Los Angeles-based studio GNUFORM (www.gnuform.com). Their work is informed by research and an experimental approach, involving the application of material dynamics to the organization of form. Payne has taught at Rice University, Pratt Institute, Bennington College, Rensselaer Polytechnic Institute, and since 2002 teaches at the UCLA Department of Architecture and Urban Design.

A conversation between Sanford Kwinter and Jason Payne

Sanford Kwinter: We met back in the mid-nineties. I was in L.A. and you came to a lecture carrying a copy of the first volume of *Artificial Life* from the Santa Fe Institute …

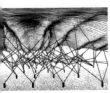

the epigenetic landscape: illustration of the gene's modulation of the landscape's form.

Jason Payne: Yeah, in the mid-90s that was the first hard core access to real Complexity theory. The paradox is that I was drawing cellular automata by hand, doing catastrophe experiments…

It was at most a physical understanding I was seeking, but I was convinced that it was the way forward; it just felt right. I remember the Waddington diagrams of the epigenetic landscape you published around then. I was fascinated by them, but didn't yet understand how to think about their architectural ramifications. It was a great time because nothing had yet congealed into an identifiable set of stylistic characteristics. It was also a scary period because of the lack of technical expertise around then. We did not yet know what to draw or how to draw it.

K: A few years later we were working together on the East Coast developing a website for an architecture school and you brought in some quite bizarre pictures of sea protoplasm…

P: … that was two male octopuses of different species having sex with one another. One was really big, light-colored and angry-looking, the other small and dark, hard to make out in the murky water. The photo was taken in 1977 on one of the very first trips down to one of those fields of black smokers in the deepest part of the Pacific. The point is that nothing like had ever been seen, and it added importantly to our awareness of the overall monstrosity of the natural environment itself. Like many in those days, I had been reading Deleuze, Georges Bataille and the Marquis de Sade. Each had written in a theoretical way about "buggery" which I found to be the height of both genius and hilarity. I know I'm not the only one of my generation to harbor a fascination with the monstrous. A lot of work one sees in California schools today looks strikingly similar to those two lovemaking octopuses!

K: How did you get from organized plasmas to the fibre spaces you showed at the *Gnuform: Hairstyle* exhibition?

P: When I first began to think about hair—hirsutism—in architecture I was only half serious: thought I'd go through the exercise of taking hairiness as seriously as possible (like the others mentioned did with buggery) and see if it could generate new principles for design, knowing there was a high likelihood that it would be merely comical. To my amazement, it yielded a number of interesting results (also plenty of laughter.) I began by researching the 'biology' of hair morphology and then, with Heather Roberge, started to develop particle animations on the computer to simulate the behavior and organization of 'hairy systems' so that we could eventuall understand how to digitally 'grow' hair. Pretty soon we were shaping hair into increasingly architectural organizations… Today we're actually known for our use of hair in projects both in terms of generative principles and as decorative motifs. We're still amazed that we actually pulled it off… our first act of architectural buggery you could say! The possibilities of hirsutery are certainly far from exhausted, but I'm now interested in finding other unsuspecting systems to sneak up behind and see what kind of offspring they can be made to produce.[1]

Man-o-war (Jason Payne and Heather Roberge of Gnuform)

K: A lot of people on the West Coast are currently pursuing the motif of 'grotesque' architecture. A quick glance from a distance suggests the extended influence of Frank Gehry...

P: I would agree that interest in the monstrous appears to be all the rage now. Greg Lynn refers to it as "monstrous indexicality."

K: The index is a category of sign in which the 'mark' is a direct (literal) result of a physical or mechanical action on a material. Like something half way between Aristotle's 'material' and 'efficient' causes, except that the index's most important feature is that it represents an unmediated and uninflected causality. Do you think it is this one-dimensional literalism that Lynn is referring to, the one typified by the cliché of Frank Gehry crumpling up a piece of paper and sending it off to the engineers to build without so much as a further thought or any systematic elaboration?

P: If I had to guess what he means by this I would say it is a form of indexical work spun in particular aesthetic direction. The term 'indexing'—another shibboleth in danger of losing descriptive potency through casual overuse, especially on the West Coast—would refer here at its most general level to generating an organization by playing one system off of another. A simple example in nature would be a seedpod; the bulging skin of the pod serves as an *index* of the pressure exerted by the seeds within.

So the term I believe refers to work that makes a central point of indexing, where displaying the indexing motif has become an end in itself. This usually means that there is a visible reciprocity between the two (or more) systems. It could be argued that first generation of "indexing" is exemplified in Peter Eisenman's work, which of course develops an even earlier kernel of indexicality drawn from Colin Rowe. The second generation—indexicality's "golden age"—came with Eisenman's offspring, with the work of people like Foreign Office Architects, Reiser+Umemoto, Greg Lynn, etc. But the third generation, the students, you might say of Eisenman's students, appears to have accepted indexing as a method unconditionally, largely without the critical perspective or the spirit of philosophical inquiry brought to it by their predecessors. With our work (sure, I include myself in this generation) it often seems that everything is indexed. It is only natural, then, that a variety of styles of indexing would emerge, of which the "monstrous" is but one. The word "grotesque" as you used it, has also been employed frequently in relation to this work but its use in my opinion is less useful than in its clear reference to a past architectural language with specific formal and spatial qualities such as heaviness, "molten" massing, high ratio of poché-to-space, undulating surfaces, deep, rich coloration, complicated plans and sections, asymmetrical composition, deep, narrow spaces, obscured construction technique, high level of decoration with ornamental references tending toward the occult, etc. Today's 'monstrous' often appears scary, with repeated elements that look like bones or other biomorphic shapes such as teeth, claws, or scales. Only shapes with a sinister or threatening appearance seem to do (flowers don't work, though occasionally carnivorous plants make an appearance.) So, among this group of third generation practitioners it has become increasingly important that the indexicality be stylistically inflected.

I think this is good because style can be a source of invention. On the other hand, this kind of—often shallow—work is virtually overwhelming many of the more important schools of architecture today. In fact, certain schools are now pumping out nothing more than the same monotonous fields of gently undulating, repeating forms, each subtly inflected by its neighbor. It's not so much that the work is bad—although it is rarely very good—it's that it is, despite the lack of quality, so *persuasive*. It's already become stultifyingly routine even before anyone has even begun to describe what it is...

SK: So what is it?

JP: At its best, I'd say the work could be described as an optimistic attempt to circumvent the representational function in architecture. For some time there has been a desire to somehow get beyond representation and meaning but to do so seems impossible because our work always involves the manipulation of signs and symbols. Indexicality is clever in that the symbols become elements or agents and meaning becomes performance or behavior. Technically we still work through representation, but it is less about making marks and more about making forms. There are two strains of indexical work currently circulating through our discourse in L.A. The first (and by far most popular) is concerned with indexing purely as image. Most of this work is derived from the AA in London and from Columbia (New York) in the 1990s, and then from SCIArc, and UCLA in more recent years. These designers and schools seem to believe that an overwhelmingly "indexed" composition is somehow an impressive or adequate reflection of what is most contemporary and therefore produce compositions that, more than anything else, strive to be *obviously* indexical (or parametric, or scripted) in aspect. This work seeks to *look* as indexical as possible as if this were a virtue in itself. Sadly, but not surprisingly, these designers talk mostly about "imageability"—how important it is for each office to have a distinct "image," etc. (there are those who seek to be "monstrously indexical," others "elegantly indexical," or "interactively indexical," etc.) These designers, primarily oriented toward appearances, rely on 2D representation (refined digital renderings) to promote their practices. Their genealogy may well run directly from Eisenman through Lynn and FOA but their motivations are very different. Although the work is not devoid of merit, I believe it is actually deliberately superficial and more than likely represents a dead end. It operates largely as a clique of ersatz (and not easily defensible) contemporaneity and is already well on its way to having been exploited and exposed beyond public tolerance.
But there is a second, obviously rarer path that interests me far more. It is one that involves the use of indexing incidentally, simply to get the job done. Indexing to produce distinct effects, indexing to connect two different systems, etc. Its use is more sparing and judicious, less naive and therefore less glorified and totalizing. "Use when necessary and then move on" type of thing. Very pragmatic. (Such "pragmatic indexicality" by the way, while deeper and representing a genuine form of research, does not leave an image any less powerful or salient than the other more superficial forms that are essentially calculated for this effect. The work of Reiser+Umemoto would be an obvious example of the second approach.)
The second tendency generates compositions that are instantly distinguishable from the first:

more heterogeneous and less one-dimensional, more nuanced and historically and culturally invested than those of the former group. Likewise, the designers in this group do not form nearly as cohesive a front as do those in the first group (they do not generally interact with one another as a defined, idiomatic "front"). Their influence over students is different as well. Average students are rarely attracted due to the absence of prescriptive formulas, but exceptional students are often attracted to the openness, difficulty and speculative aspects of it. This 'school', still underground but clearly having an impact on its more visible counterpart, makes predominant use of 3D models, especially physical ones. There is less emphasis on rendering skills and they frequently eschew animation altogether. You won't see them scripting anything except as a last resort. This group's genealogy doubtless seems more complicated, even contradictory, with lines running through Reiser+Umemoto and

Lynn but also through Miralles and Eisenman and even, paradoxically perhaps, Libeskind. These practices include Ruy-Klein, in which mixtures of advanced parametric logics and arcane manual tradecrafts (such as embroidery) blend to produce uncanny compositions that are not quite synthetic and not quite natural. Rhett Russo stirs parametric connections into even more idiosyncratic selections of low-tech substrate to create projects that studiously avoid digital cliché. Lawrence Blough of Graftworks uses clever mixtures of various "abstract" geometries with the more prosaic realities of construction and building materials. In a slightly different vein are the subtle approaches of Ferda Kolatan and Erich Schoenenberger of su11, in which the work sails deliberately close to the parametric wind but resists the totalizing applications of these softwares by using non-parametric methods,

Hanging stair (Lawrence Blough of Graftworks)

strong programming and contextual sensitivity. I view su11's work as a kind of resistance from within. What distinguishes these practices is their understanding that parametrics are not forms but simply relations between forms—obvious perhaps, but rare in current production. These designers, and their far deeper understanding of indexicality and parametrics, will ultimately rule the day.

Indexing does seem to be our innate lens for seeing the world—the oscillations and interactions of indexical composition are native to us; they derive from our historical experience with certain kinds of electronic music, rave culture, ecstasy, videos, and video games. We are well aware that we have not yet managed to make a fundamental contribution. It doesn't take a lot to realize that much of the reason probably lies with our generation's general distaste for intellectual gravity, our satisfaction with liteness, our lack of political or revolutionary commitment, even our lack of concern with our own history. (This arguably has to do with being so steeped in a culture of irony—it's not that we aren't intellectually serious, but more that we don't entirely trust it.) On the other hand, I'd say we have failed to recognize that the volumetric elements—the bones, teeth, claws, and scales I referred to earlier that characterize some of the new indexical work—*represent a major breakthrough* of a kind! One could say that these represent the beginnings of a physical, material rewriting of what otherwise has remained merely diagrammatic. I'd say this is what currently distinguishes the second from the third generation of practitioners, the awareness on the part of the older group of the potential role of matter to propel this work forward. For example, FOA's use of specific angles of repose in the landscape to create a variety of programmatic possibilities in their project for the Coastal Park in Barcelona, or Reiser + Umemoto's tracking the movement of the utility core by the density of window mullions in their Sagaponac House are each examples of real material organizations created through indexing with real material elements. You said it yourself once in a lecture: "matter is the new space." As I see it, our generation has found two ways forward on this theme. We either take up the pragmatic realism of the second generation and think in terms of architectural elements, or we weight the more abstract volumes we seem to like so much with the physics of substance and mass *so that we can begin to build with them.* Either way requires a much more serious incorporation of matter into the work.

SK: The "matter" question as you note has been a fundamental one to me as well. And yes, it has been disconcerting to hear emerging designers and teachers in recent years, mouthing the same jargon from 12 and 15 years ago only now, the second time round, disconnected from any discernable historical or intellectual substrate—as if it were suddenly now only a parochial architectural issue, in fact a drafting issue at that. There is an often terrifying predominance of 'shop talk' and endless waxing about things like scripting as if entire arguments were somehow bundled up within the word itself, but which no one in the sect is willing (or able) to divulge… I suppose that I would be classified among your 'second generation' practitioners. I would remind you that there is considerable encroachment of 'third generational' postures in our ranks as well. But certainly no one talks about things like scripting as if it were anything more than a drafting technicality. Our generation was in love with ideas and their extensions, not techniques. How did the shift come about?

JP: I have some ideas about that. But it's worth asking what role technical developments have played, since so many practices place these so centrally in their projects. "Scripting" for example, is a very simple thing: an efficient way to produce differentiated repetition in digital modeling that would otherwise require a great deal of time and effort. At its essence it is a method for reducing the number of keystrokes required to model, alter, and then repeat a particular form. There is no mystery behind it and it is, contrary to myth, easy to learn (dangerously easy in fact—it's where the term "Maya monkeys" comes from.) It is a powerful tool for modeling and an important technical skill for the digital designer to possess. As I said I strongly believe that its use should be backgrounded to a supporting role in contemporary indexical work. Through scripting it is possible to produce so much material so fast that

ripted product almost always overwhelms the scene, forcing all else out. On a superficial
vel this frequently generates good-looking images because most scripted compositions
ppear *full*. They also appear coherent and cohesive due to the finely calibrated change in
ach repeated form. All of this of course is quite deceiving since it represents a largely random
esture with a huge (automatic) computational response. The fullness I mentioned leaves no
om for any architectural element not able to be produced through scripting, nor does it leave
om for the inevitable thickening that occurs during materialization. Similarly, the coherence
nd cohesion, being of a rarefied and exotic nature, often do not mix well with disparate and
uotidian elements so often required in realistic architectural proposals. I feel very strongly
bout this so when I script (which is rare) I try to bury the scripted material within layers of
nscripted composition.

K: There is no doubt that the same economic logic—efficiency—that favors extending
ngle design gestures over exponentially larger expanses of space, as in most new suburban
evelopments especially in the developing world (Asia, South Asia, the American sunbelt, etc.),
 also at work in the popularization of this new technique. It represents an impoverishment
at has become routine in our culture and needs no explanation. Yet everyone remembers when
artoon animation was first rationalized and routinized and became no longer the product
f the hand: the plasticity and movement of the space and its objects became so poor and
iminished that one had to listen rather than watch in order to be engaged by, or move along
ith, the narrative and its forms. And then suddenly, yet after a very long time, movement of an
xtraordinarily beautiful and nuanced sort returned to the screen, largely thanks to the digital
nnovations of Pixar and their followers. Surely this suggests that the techniques are not solely to
lame for the ugliness and clumsiness of contemporary architectural production, it is the minds
nd worldviews of those who are developing and using them that need to be explained.

P: Absolutely. The shift is from substance to image and definitely corresponds to generational
alues. In my view, while each generation is largely continuous with its predecessor, each
 also largely conditioned by its original experience of architecture and of life, the former
ccurring during their education. The "second generation" began their education during
 rather rich transition from modernity to postmodernity that was characterized by a kind of
isciplinary "exfoliation"; as the discourse moved toward postmodernity in its various guises
 opened itself more than ever before to a variety of external influences: philosophy, literary
riticism, mathematics, the sciences, etc. The field seemed more fertile than ever before,
pen to new growth through new ideas, techniques, and mediums. The second generation
ventually coalesced into a group ultimately concerned with form and geometry but these
ere forms and geometries strongly connected to outside influences. Even today you find these
esigners far more adept at moving from architecture's formal interiority to speculations on
ore worldly ramifications. By contrast, the "third generation" is largely mired in a kind of
isconnected expertise in form- and image-making. By the time we entered architecture school,
ostmodernism was defunct and deconstructivism had flared out as a bankrupt mishandling
f philosophical ideas that ultimately proved too complex for simple representational

appropriation. We saw both the beauty of these projects and their obvious superficiality vis-à-vis deconstruction, and I believe this led to a certain cynicism regarding the role of conceptual underpinnings for advanced architecture. The transition from Derrida to Deleuze occurred shortly thereafter, coinciding with the dramatic rise of digital processes. The concept of Deleuze meshed well with an emerging digital idiom ("smooth and striated," "rhizome," "folding," etc.) making deeper interpretations of this strain of poststructuralist thought unnecessary. My sense is that the "second generation" saw Deleuzian thought as a natural, more optimistic *conceptual* foundation for the evolution of experimental architecture, while the "third generation" viewed Deleuze's landscape of metaphors far more literally, knowing they could build the kind of catchphrase terms listed above in new and elegant ways using advanced software. This has played out as a relatively a-critical cavalcade of folds and rhizomes, both smooth and striated, over the past 15 years or so.

SK: There is no doubt that what you call the 'third generation'—one hopes not a definitively lost generation—not only have a distaste for attaching thought and argument to their work, but rely on incomplete understandings of the arguments and thoughts that they claim to presuppose in the work of their predecessors and teachers. This point was convincingly made by Reiser and Umemoto in their *Atlas of Novel Tectonics*; they took a third of the book to decry the laziness and disingenuousness of the following generation. And they could have been far more brutal. (Van Berkel and Bos offer the same criticisms in their *Design Models: Architecture, Urbanism, Infrastructure*.) But what is particularly strange is to find a generation without a discourse at all aside from metaphors and vague pronouncements about 'effects' copped from TV and campy films. For my own part, I have found small practices of greater humility such as Aranda and Lasch, who don't generally make forms that people want to imitate, of far greater interest than the latest generation of Playboys (to cite Gideon as I did when describing the soulless output of the second generation several years ago). Terraswarm's (Aranda/Lasch) work is essentially laboratory research, with a genuine heuristic drive. When they did their billboard project in Brooklyn last year it may have bored the third generation playboys, but it constituted a breakthrough that neither the MIT nor the Penn school had been able to achieve: they applied algorithmic 'machines' to color and light and demonstrated that they had deeper insight than others about how instructions (universally) determine form. They made the rest of the 'third' or emerging generation seem depressingly parochial by comparison. Likewise when they used video-mounted birds to 'cursor' the city below they were approaching the dictum that sustained me through the '90s, to "let matter model matter". . . For me the litmus test in all this is who really believes in nature of nature (the "logic of the living" as François Jacob called it) and who's imagination is limited to making amusing pictures of it. Another example is the research of Achim Menges (at Offenbach and the AA) who derives all his experiments from the concrete world of materials loaded with forces and uses the software environment to capture the geometries that the real world produces and to subject them to systematics in the same way that second generation practitioners might. He naturally speaks about a 'physiology' of forms in the same way as a biologist: because he has a purchase on actual behaviors—and not only fantasies of behaviors—he can operate on matter in a way not dissimilar to the meshworks of nature.

His forms are resultants, not of crude literalisms like 'indexes' but of 'logics' and algorithmic machines: a "Darwinian machine" that strives to innovate and a "Bernardian machine" (after Claude Bernard) that seeks to restore equilibrium (or homeostasis). Because he has understood that form is an exfoliation of logic—not force—he may be alone to have any claim to being a materialist in the end. His forms invariably begin in the world, get processed in the parametric environment and are redelivered—and tested—in the world. So I think there is very strong justification to doubt the continuity of the third generation with the first and second except in very few limited cases. Something fundamental is being lost in the transition in most.

P: To speculate on differences in generational sensibility deriving from worldview and life experience is obviously tricky, fraught with assumptions and generalizations that could never apply to every specific case. Nevertheless, I do believe that each generation is, to a degree, distinct from the others for reasons well beyond differences in education and disciplinary history. Generations X and Y are often described in terms of their unique cultural influences such as the rise of music videos and video gaming, the proliferation of sub-genres of all kinds (especially in our musical forms,) the absence of wars in which we are directly engaged (such as Vietnam for the boomers) and most interestingly for me, our particular predilections with respect to drugs. All of these, I would argue, would lead to interesting and useful observations on what makes our generation distinct, but it is the latter the strikes me as perhaps the most revealing of all. It is here that one can grasp something essential in our particular understanding of what architecture should be and do.

Very regularly a particular drug rises above the level of general recreational use to capture a larger moment in time, a *zeitgeist*, and as such becomes symbolic of the feel of its time. In the late eighties and nineties that drug was arguably ecstasy (MDMA). Like cocaine in the eighties or acid in the sixties, ecstasy rose to prominence alongside the whole sensibility of a generation. I like to refer to the distinction as *the ecstatic vs. the acidic* because my observations on ecstasy's impact on the development of a generational sensibility relies on its comparison to the impact LSD had on the '68 generation. The primary difference between the action of the two drugs involves the perceived location of the high itself: acid is "felt" most profoundly in the mind whereas ecstasy "feels" more distributed *throughout the body*. An acid trip tends to be an alienating experience, turning the user inward toward an exploration of "inner space." Observations and experiences while on acid tend to be cerebral in nature, with users reporting revelations involving the rationalization of life and experience. Ecstasy, on the other hand, generates deep feelings of connectedness with others and is famous for producing a poignant set of physical desires, all pleasurable, from thumb-sucking and jaw-clenching to powerful compulsions toward physical contact with others in the form of hugging, massage, close dancing (usually during raves,) and even sex. To put it simply, acid tends to enhance *thought* while ecstasy encourages *feel*. Acid is *cerebral* while ecstasy is *nervous*.

Whether today's young architects actually took these generational drugs of choice during their formative years is mostly irrelevant—there exists nonetheless the universality of knowledge of these substances in their broader culture. In the late sixties as in the nineties, both drugs fueled the growth of their own cultural cosmoses, driving new developments in music, fashion, art, film, psychology, and even law and politics. To listen to the acid-amplified brilliance of Hendrix's guitar is to have a momentary taste of his transcendent technical intelligence regarding the limits of the electric guitar just as losing oneself to the collective, writhing trance of an over-crowded rave approaches the effects of actual MDMA intoxication. Given this, I suspect that the icy-cold alienation and fierce precision in the early work of "paper architects" like Eisenman and Hedjuk was somehow reflective of the acidic atmosphere of the time. That work was *thought* rather than *felt*, at least in its first moves, with any feel that might emerge being secondary. I am similarly convinced that the conceptual depth of the "second generation" has been largely conditioned by this commitment to the primacy of the cerebellum over the nervous system if for no other reason than the lack of a new drug during the eighties to force a shift in consciousness and culture (cocaine, while clearly popular after acid and before ecstasy, simply does not produce mind-altering effects of the magnitude necessary to shift cultural awareness and atmosphere in the same way.)

The rise of MDMA use and its wide cultural impact during the nineties produced what I would call an *ecstatic sensibility*, an atmosphere entirely different from its predecessors. You see this in music in the shift from lyric-based songs attempting to convey message to sound-based songs preoccupied with feel. In architecture, focus shifted from cerebral ratiocination to physical sensation, but this transition has not been entirely smooth or coherent. There was no singular moment at which my generation consciously decided to move toward this new sensibility for calculated reasons. Instead, much of the shift has occurred due to ambivalence toward— and ignorance of—historical lineage as well as the transformation in thinking and technique brought about by digital tools.

Beyond this putative shift from the cerebral to the nervous, there are other parallels that are likely connected to ecstatic sensibility. MDMA is synthetic and much was made of this shift to "designer drugs" when ecstasy first came on the recreational scene. Prior to MDMA, drugs were understood to be one-of-a-kind substances: marijuana was marijuana, cocaine was cocaine, etc. (This, despite varietal strains of the organics and different preparations possible with most drugs.) MDMA, on the other hand, is but one member of a large family of phenethylamines that includes hundreds of other related psychotropic compounds, each with its own feel. The proliferation of the phenethylamines continues to frustrate drug enforcement agencies because each one must be legislated in turn. (For a fascinating trip through the different colors and flavors of these compounds see Alexander and Ann Shulgin's classic *PIHKAL*, an acronym standing for "Phenethylamines I Have Known And Loved.") Due to the ease of recombination to create new drugs, "designer drugs" such as ecstasy became known not so much as singular compounds with fixed identities but rather as a distributed field of related effects. Some are more visual than others, some more "feely," some cooler and some warmer, some are noticeably "tingly" sending pleasurable chills through the body throughout the trip while others only send the classic "onset chill" once in the beginning, some feel distinctly sexual while others feel platonic, some are quite speedy while others more lethargic. These are nuanced differences and we are comfortable with the delicacy of distinction required to connoisseur these substances.

We have in turn become highly attuned, even finely tuned, like the engines in temperamental British sports cars. For this reason we feel that the perceived self-similarity in our design work is a misperception by outside critics not so attuned to sensing subtle difference. Some designers within our "clique," as you call it, seem especially committed to differences so fine they resist perception even by their peers (the work of Hernan Diaz-Alonzo at SCIArc, for example seems indistinguishably similar to itself in every iteration—even I (an avid and close reader of this train of work) find it difficult to tell them apart. My own taste is to strive for much greater distinction in general—both within and between projects—both a function of, and the reason for, a far lower reliance on parametric software as well as a general distaste for closed systems.

A further important characteristic of the ecstatic is its "speediness." MDMA tends to heighten awareness rather than dull it (as do the opiates, marijuana, and alcohol) and ecstasy is often cut with amphetamine, to increase its speed even more. Speediness is actually a combination of two effects that blend nicely: a compulsion toward increased activity and euphoria. When you are properly "speeding" you are feeling more than just fast, you are feeling *good* and fast. Much third generation work feels good and fast. Fast generally means an excess of elements (say, hundreds rather than dozens) and *good* fast work displays exuberant excess. Some designers achieve exuberance through the flamboyance of individual components which, when repeated over and over achieve a powerful sense of fertility. I use this strategy as well but never in isolation; for me, blooms of activity are best rooted in more stable soils, a lesson I learned when working with Jesse Reiser and Nanako Umemoto. (Other contemporaries of mine work this way as well: David Ruy and Karel Klein of Ruy-Klein Architecture, Lawrence Blough of Graftworks, etc.) Speediness is a hallmark quality of third generation desire.

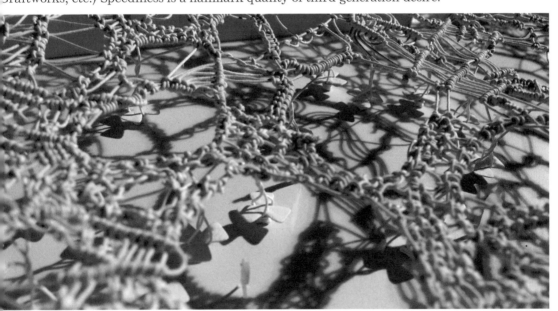

Ruy KleinArchitecture, 2007. PS1 Competition Entry (Finalist)

Of course, the adage that "speed kills" is true, and there is clear risk when over-amping architectural compositions. I call this "redlining". Its a form of death by acceleration or overdose that has become common, and to which scripters are the most prone. It happens when the work becomes nothing other than a restless, compulsive accumulation of parts. The workspace becomes so overfull and overwrought that everything—program, structure, space—is squeezed out. So enamored of algorithmic flow, speed freaks either forget or ignore the prosaic concreteness of architecture's pragmatics. Embarrassing arguments as to "alternative functionality" are offered after the fact but don't come close to salvaging a broader efficacy and relevance for work which is essentially as meaningless as the worst '70s formalism.

SK: I'm not indifferent to your fantastic arguments, although I'd say they're more seductive than comprehensively convincing. There is no doubt in my mind that affective worlds present as wholes in which all parts determine one another. Your emphasis on 'experience' I've long argued, is an inadvertent—and interesting—recidivism of your generation, yet not necessarily a regression. While our generation and the one that preceded ours made done with phenomenologies, yours has turned to it as if 50 years of philosophical emancipation never happened. I remember the first time I was in a classroom and was struck to the quick by a comment that made me jettison a considerable amount of faith in "history": it was 1991 and a student evoked an emerging band called Nirvana as having introduced a new type of affect into our culture that was seeking a response in architecture that simply did not pre-exist but rather needed to be made. I knew Nirvana slightly, but had no sense yet of how utterly fundamental they were (that student already did). Without understanding it exactly, I knew she was right, or at least potentially right. But if affects are historical, one ought to be as nuanced as possible in thinking about them. We used to contrast the urban 'speed' scene and music of the '60s to the more 'bucolic' atmosphere of pot and the psychedelics (think Velvet Underground vs. the Doors or protest music). Certainly it felt convincing; at any rate these WERE two different worlds and they did not for the most part meet. I myself experienced the 1990s very differently from you. I remember this period beginning with the revival of psychedelic utopias associated with the rise of electronic interfaces and cyberculture: virtual reality for example began as a political, psychic and erotic ideal, especially through journals like *Mondo 2000*. It was the first glimmer of a revival of a counterculture: genuine, but brief. Soon after, a so-called new 'psychedelic underground' emerged strongly associated with the emerging sciences of chaos, complexity, dynamical systems theory, a smattering of hindu-buddhist ethics and cosmology, and a strong connection to nature and computational metaphysics. There was also the typographic revolution associated with surfer culture that found its most eloquent exponent in the magazines and graphics of David Carson. A whole new approach to letterforms, photography, image culture and lifestyle had emerged, California-based, and without a doubt neurochemically assisted. (To say that the 'acid' era was gone, would be a true mistake; it had simply found a new context and mood to live in.) In any case the Nirvana argument certainly had resonance with these simultaneous developments (distress, for example was a predominant affect in both music and typography...) The neurochemistry associated with this era actually had much more to lo with the legendary molecule DMT (Dimethyltriptamine), the anthropological lore around ayahuasca, ethnobotany, psylocibin, neurochemicals that allowed one to experience vast correlations within one's own body, to experience one's own physical body as intelligent, as mind, as a cascade of information within matter, the same features that one was beginning to be able to study in computational realms and in nature at large. It was a period when the transformations in knowledge that were arriving allowed one to conceive of oneself not as IN the world but AS the world itself. (DMT was famously a drug that Harvard's ethnobotany department demonstrated to be capable of producing "collective hallucinations" in which entire groups would somehow see the same things.) Yes, there was a wave of epistemological and ethical holism that helped drive perception and research and by extension that drove design. It culminated in a deep belief in algorithms as the new units of the 'real'. Algorithms were connected to experience, sensibility, aesthetics AND research. In any case, it was the context in which we, at least, were reading the papers of the Santa Fe Institute. Computers played a role only until around 1992. By the time the first Silicon Graphics machines arrived on the design scene computers had already become peripheral to the developments that were really interesting. Unfortunately, many architects got connected at just that moment, while others who were already moving with the new developments, lost their direction and became fatally distracted by computers rather than by computation. The real issue is algorithmic complexity as a new model of matter, form and behavior on a general scale. It meant many ideas had to change. Today it is hard to find ideas at all in the new work, let alone an acknowledgment that relations between things have changed and that there are a million new things to learn and make. The argument of about feelings is fine (if effete sounding to my generation) but it doesn't account for history. My take on the history of the body in the 1990s is quite different the one you propose: I see your third generation as having lost its connection to the material substrate in which the mind works, exiled within an equipment-saturated world, sold on the hype of cyberfreedom and cybersociality and compensating wildly with ersatz realities like 'special effects'. A whole generation of designers today thinks that design cues should be taken from movie production! The DMT world is a world of total interconnection and feedback, so compressed that information, movement and matter—and the nervous system—are indistinguishable from one another. I still see this—what I used to call 'wet' computation—as the way to outlive the now defunct 'computer revolution'. In the '90s, I would argue, the mystery of the body was revealed to us as a product of ancient organized forces that we started to name with new names like 'attractors', 'basins' and 'chreods'. The affects of the body were linked not just to forms but to the active forms that gave forms and that connected everything present to what is oldest and most primitive in matter. This is what a DMT excursion shows you in the most explosive and dense way. Its like a trip into Darwinian past AND into the chemistry of one's flesh at the same time. (It is said to be the most intense experience the nervous system can experience and it involves both psychedelic visions and intense ideation.) Perhaps its most important feature of all is the insight of cohesiveness that it produces. In today's 'third generation' discourse this ideational dimension is gone. Many designers think forms come out of computers or movies.

JP: While this is certainly true of some, it is not true of all. For the most part I'd say it's a result of a parallax view: digital terrain is not native to older generations of critics and observers and a just evaluation requires close reading. The two schools I am describing have their own distinguishing nuances.

I too remember the moment in 1991 when Nirvana burst onto the scene, and I could well have been that student you refer to for I had the same sense that the new sound would force a larger cultural reckoning. When *Rolling Stone Magazine* interviewed Cobain I was struck by the way he explained both his vocal affect and his approach to writing lyrics. He commented that he sang from his upper abdomen, just below the breastbone, because "…that's where I scream, that's where I feel…" Vocal coaches will tell you that this method is technically incorrect and even harmful over the long term. Cobain surely didn't care, his misuse of the vocal instrument was the only way for him to convey the grinding, guttural sound that was, for him, meaning. As another *Rolling Stone* writer (Chris Mundy) observed of this shift toward affective rather than lyrical communication that "…the medium is the message." There was a politics to grunge but no distinct "message," and that was intentional. It would impact culture through other means, through the power of mood, effect, and posture. It was NOT a nihilistic turning away from the political dimension of rock, but rather an attempt to move past earlier, lyrical forms of communication that these artists felt had become exhausted. What the third generation architects are doing now is not dissimilar to this. I don't expect you'd describe Nirvana or early Smashing Pumpkins as "effete". Similarly, I find your comment about phenomenology hard to make sense of. I'm advocating work that appeals directly to the senses. In the end what matters is architecture's efficacy…what it *does*. Architecture, history shows, is often capable of building images of thought, and we also know that architecture sometimes aims for a more direct influence on life. A commitment to the latter can disrupt the representational clarity of the former. Right now we are seeing a clash between these two fundamental motivations playing out not only in the work of the third generation but in the second as well. Your account of the influence of complexity on architecture illustrates this well, and it is true that most experimental, digitally-oriented design has become mired in what you call an equipment (and software) saturated world. These designers, some knowingly and some not, are consumed with mere representations of technology, complexity, and computation. While I find this project weak and uninteresting, I recognize that it *is* a project and is, in some way, connected to representational work of the past (for example, the stillborn, high steroid, "high tech" movement of the eighties, not a pretty picture either then or now). On the other hand, I do not feel so unsympathetic to the original "machine aesthetic' work of the early century: the initial appeal to aircraft, automobiles, and machines in general quickly evolved endemic forms and made this inspirational material *native to architecture:* clean lines, taut skins, and fearless expression of function was more a product of the era's architecture than the machines themselves. Architects simply borrowed the desire and made it their own. The very best digital today work seeks this same kind of durability through disciplinary responsibility.

K: If phenomenology means nothing to the emerging generation, I'd say this was more a liability than a virtue: it effectively leaves them without a framework to discuss experience, or a model to produce and modulate it with work. For my own part, I return to phenomenology more and more in my teaching these days; I make an effort to show why it failed and has been so denigrated in the course of 20th century thought, but then show how contemporary developments, especially in neurology, have the potential to redeem many aspects of it. One of the primary doctrines of neurology is that the mind can best be understood from the study of its pathological states, rather than its healthy or 'normal' ones. This on its own provides a framework for thinking about what you call 'affective' states: in any case it saves it from the impressionism and neo-connoisseurship that is becoming a hallmark of the third generation's discourse. In other words, pathology produces *organized disturbances*; even the classical 20th century model of aphasia produced or described 'poetic' products as possessing a systematic intelligibility. That's what poetics is. Likewise with the model of evolutionary psychology: it offers a framework to explain states of mind, and especially capacities of mind in relation to form, and as responses to environmental pressures of the evolutionary past. It may even explain what you call 'effects'. In the 1960s some psychologists used to speak of "aesthetic fright": an example is the baboon's, or certain birds' fear of serpentine forms that they KNOW are not real snakes. Current work-thought constellations in architecture do not provide much room for anything but expressions of taste and usually campy taste at that. Some have tried to revive 'beauty' as a criterion of judgment, as if we were back in the 19th century salons of provincial town-dwellers who had never visited Paris but affected to adopt (what they thought were) its attitudes nonetheless. Once systematics goes out the window, there is no limit to how far things can regress.

In addition to this foreclosure of criteria, the foreclosure of concepts with which to grasp, extend and develop the work, there is that certain poverty that you have noted to exist in the products themselves. This probably has to do with the profound error into which a generation is now falling, which is to have mistaken parametric software and scripting techniques as "design" tools when they are not this, but only realization or resolution tools. Jesse Reiser is fond of remarking how Michelangelo classified weaving at the bottom of the scale of the arts—with nothing lower—presumably because it represented the simple playing out of a one-dimensional algorithm or instruction by a single gesture (of the shuttle) repeated a thousand times (he considered weavers to verge on imbecility). The production of cloth here is of course not of the tapestry variety, but that of the simple repeated pattern. Clearly the effect you began by describing as a benchmark of compelling design, what I would suggest calling here the 'dialogical' effect in which more than one set of instructions is played off of the others (although the two superimposed systems of indexical design seems a very poor understanding of this) is a dealbreaker for the strong advocate of the script. Anyone with a passing acquaintance with renaissance art has encountered the well-noted deadness of Piero della Francesca's painting of The Ideal City. They will also know Masaccio's radical Christ in The Holy Trinity: for Masaccio taught painters how to use perspective by realizing that it could not be applied rotely as it was in the Piero. Scientific perspective, literally applied, killed the space and the life of the painting; it had to be used, as you said of scripting, in the background, in piecemeal manner and with judicious restraint. One experiences the same thing when looking at the works that come out of studios in our so-called best schools: once you've got past the strained forms, a poverty of both the senses and the sensibility hits one (a poverty that goes beyond the mindlessness of the forms, but is actually a property of their counterfeit nature, as they try to pass themselves off as 'matter' or 'life', when in fact they are only movie sets for films and action stars that will never come…) I also am unable to agree that second generation computer architecture is all that much to be proud of. I often find the input of engineers—generally directed by constraints and goals—to be the only thing of real interest in works generated in these ways. Have you never noted that the work coming from European schools is so much more sophisticated these days than the American work for the first time in decades? Is it because the parametrics and the scripts are modulated and deployed within a much more crowded—and therefore overlapping and constrained—social, intellectual, historical and sensual environment? The tabula rasa fallacy is available only to the American psyche…

JP: If phenomenology is re-emerging as a potential framework for this idiom, it's probably because it coincides with the shift (still underway) from process to product. For a long time, technique and process were, in themselves, the endgame of much of the younger digital work. A few years ago many of us became frustrated with this misguided goal and became more vocal about shifting the stakes of the game. At first most of the dialogue concerned very discrete "effects" as being sufficient products of the work, but now we're advocating a more comprehensive attempt to create entire environments, atmospheres, and sensibilities that are more layered and complex. Direct appeals to phenomenological ideals are not likely to occur in the foreseeable future, but "lower," more carnal and nervous phenomena such as the pathologies you mention may be found useful. 'Low' is currently of topical interest, and is in no way inferior to 'high'. While the shift from process to product in digital work and the indexing school is gaining momentum, the more hard-core parametric designers (including the ultra-rarefied algorithmic, or scripting camp) are slower to change course. Parametric design requires a high level of technical expertise that takes years to master. What we are seeing today with parametric and scripting software is no different from the missteps architects made in the mid-90s when they mistook means for ends and ended up fetishizing software environments like SoftImage, Alias and Maya. But I don't view this as catastrophically as you do; I view it as a kind of training that prepares for later, more comprehensive and mature performances. At any rate, the aim is to get beyond the process obsession of the '80s and '90s. I am optimistic for two reasons: first, the awareness, intelligence, and commitment to real product on the part of leading practitioners I've mentioned earlier, and second, the increasing volume of criticism from above. You are not the only one to decry what you perceive as a lack of focus on the part of the third generation. In recent years even those who've been sympathetic to our work have raised concern (this includes Eisenman himself, Jeff Kipnis, Sylvia Lavin, Greg Lynn, Jesse Reiser, etc.) I have faith that advanced digital design in general and parametrics in particular will find its way out of the bramble of technical savantism toward a more healthy, robust, and pragmatic deployment.

.K: As you know I find the ideas that have transformed thinking about form over the last decades to be extremely beautiful, and the work done in their name to be rarely satisfying (indeed often ugly and simplistic). Among the notable exceptions to this was the formulation of Ben van Berkel in the late '90s. Its simplicity was the most astonishing thing of all and he used it as the title of an article: "The Box AND the Blob". UNStudio's ability to invent is largely a result of the intellectual flexibility they opened up for themselves with formulations of just this type, the recognition that nature creates its machines from everything it has at hand and integrates them into working wholes. The American school is often unable to find this sophistication in its processes, since it is highly technocratic and obsessed with promotion through theoretical innovation. Now that you make an argument for your generation's interest in the 'real' as opposed to the speculative, one might expect a similar increase in sophistication. But the opposite has been true. The output has become increasingly strained and desperate for effect (indeed 'effects' is one of their favorite terms, as if their legitimate business was to be creating 'special effects' that find success in cinema only because they vanish from the screen within a few instants of their appearance and thus never need to survive the scrutiny of an intelligent minute...). I do believe the 'indexicality' you are speaking of is a remnant from the 1970s and should have been put to rest as among the worst of the literalisms that have plagued architecture in recent decades, yet I confess to finding the issue of repeated elements or modules a step beyond this. The latter 'parti' is one whose allure I do not actually understand, but it is one in which I am far more certain there is something useful to understand or to find. Parametric software and the script-generated continuums of contemporary digital work have a material quality of which something physical as well as metaphysical could be said. What I used to call the "parametric blanket" (largely because these works resemble a featureless blanket thrown over a highly articulated traditional workshop model) has nonetheless a materiality that could sustain discussion, a history that is at the very least interesting (dating, no doubt, from Kipnis's and Shirdel's work at the AA in the early 1990s) and some precedents in meshwork that have a rich etiology (Reiser and Umemoto). At the same time there is an almost complete flouting of the cybernetic dictum that information can be defined as "a difference that makes a difference". The current work appears to show no interest in such second order differences: indeed it eschews nearly all information of the standard kind. Is the contemporary period one in which there is a deep suspicion or antipathy to form?

JP: At its most basic, parametric design represents a deep commitment to a geometrical project as the centerpiece for architectural evolution. While geometry has often been central to architecture, it has not *always* been so. The architect's faith in geometry waxes and wanes through history and my generation has consciously accepted and extended geometry's primacy from our immediate predecessors. For this reason, our work, at least as far as it relates to architecture's interior, is largely an *extension* of that of the prior generation. Some have remarked that this seemingly uncritical acceptance of an established model for design leads to mannerism and that we have succumbed to it. But I would argue that the deep cultural pull of an ecstatic sensibility prevents such stagnation. For while the third generation takes as given much of the same material as the second, its interest in it is for entirely different reasons.

You could say that the second generation's appeal to geometry was largely a reactionary return to architecture's interior, a turning away from the pastiches of postmodernism while the third generation optimistically embraces geometry not as an act of resistance, but as an opportunistic movement forward. While they played defense (and we are grateful for it) we now play offence. Our unique lens for processing this material will inevitably push our work away from what has come before, seen already in calls for a "new phenomenology" to address our compulsion toward sensation, atmosphere, and affect.

Further, our appeal to the "lite" and the "low" (in contrast to our predecessors' reliance on more traditionally "high" forms of thought) is not anti-intellectual: many of us accept a "base materialism" as our primary mode of operation. Much of MDMA's impact has been through its commonality and inclusiveness (we *all* get it and it was able to infiltrate the larger culture—music, clothes, hairstyle, mannerisms, etc.). Ours is a deliberate shift from high to low and therefore there is less interest in announcing scholarly foundations (which run through Lucretius, Nietzsche, Bataille, Bergson, Deleuze, etc.).

SK: Parametric tools are doubtless among the most powerful computational devices yet to be put at the service of architectural production. But parametric software is not design software and its use as such has failed to produce objects or worlds of interest, novelty or depth. The charm of the many automatic processes embedded in it is undeniable but this has led many designers into the production of debilitating clichés. (It is rare to meet someone who does not express deep boredom at viewing its products in the schools, even those who produce them in their own work. The observation that it "all looks the same" has become universal.) This did not have to be the case. Most of all, the recent turn away from concepts, ideas, theories and systematics in general (toward the values you list above) have meant that architecture is now failing to draw advantage from the new (and often spectacular) ideas coming out of the sciences of form. For example, there is a new type of systematics that is being studied in genetics today known as "modularity" which may well turn out to provide some of the most powerful keys to understanding the emergence of hierarchical structures in complex forms. Modularity is pure design theory, and utterly accessible to experimentation and manipulation with design software. It operates on units and causes vertical 'decomposition' of series' of units (this is Herbert Simon's word, and modularity is one of the last things he wrote about before he died) into differentiated functions, roles and developments. The separations are like integrated divergences and allow for very rich matrices to arise, indeed everything that characterizes forms that support a wide variety of behaviors and performances. Another is 'popplulation thinking', a term borrowed from evolutionary theory, but which shows how speciation might arise from a continuum of highly similar—or even effectively identical—units. A third important idea ignored by those who claim to be interested primarily in 'affect' is the supposedly central problem of 'emergence' and 'catastrophe' (understood of course in the sense of appearance as discontinuity). Even in Goethe's algorithmic imagination he could 'decompose' complicated botanical forms into superposed interacting gradients (very different from indexicality and in fact a litmus test in the form-theoretical world). He generated more interesting plant forms with his pencil, his eye and his innate mastery of systematics in the form f intuition than the digital products one sees today, indeed since Saarinen's TWA Terminal erhaps. My feeling is not that parametrics represents a false path, its that the new generation as the wrong tool if they are truly interested in atmospheres and moods. What we have to ament is an anti-intellectualism and a sterility that uses software and connoisseurship as an libi and a foil. But there can never be an important architecture devoid of ideas.

P: The beauty and promise of emerging parametric work lies in its potential to be materialized n real structures, in both its *inflection* and its *complexion*. *Inflection* involves a specific hing's ability to swerve away from other things to become itself (I cite here Lucretius' notion f the "clinamen" or atomic swerve that produces difference, in order to further underscore materialist intention for this work). All parametric material is inflected through an ttached physics, either real or imagined (in the case of work that remains within a digital nedium) making it fundamentally different from the diagrammatic indexing that came efore. This requires some explanation: when the diagram is understood as primary and irtual (lacking physicality) then matter becomes secondary and complacent. Materiality is nerely wrapped around, or laid over, an underlying organizational armature that is somehow nderstood as free of the lowly material constraints and frictions of the real, a form of idealism ou could say. My own model tries to posit matter as organizer: matter first, organization econd. This model for architectural composition requires a different mindset of the designer. nstead of understanding the basic ingredients of architectural composition—points, lines, nd planes—as empty vessels for extrinsic values, affiliations, and meanings, this material s conceptually reframed as *intrinsically motivated* and *full*. Points, lines, and planes come aden with distinct qualities in measurable quantities such as density, pull, drag, tension, ompression, acceleration, and porosity. These qualities and quantities, or *properties*, allow eometry to become behavioral and active rather than representational and passive. In this pproach the designer no longer develops geometry for what it draws but for what it does. Jpending the traditional organization-matter relationship in this way, takes place through a rocess called "rewriting," and it is this move that I think you are responding to with optimism. Rewriting is a term from Artificial Life. I first came across it in the work of computational otanist Przemyslaw Prusinkiewicz's work on L-Systems, relatively standard subject matter or those studying complexity. L-Systems are rule-based systems designed to create branching norphologies. In order to give area, volume, and mass to otherwise dimensionless branching ystems (as when approximating leaf growth) Prusinkiewicz "rewrites" the featureless branch, r line, with a simple shape. This entails simply removing or overwriting the line with a ounded area or volume. Doing this over and over creates the artificial approximation of a rowing plant, especially when the rewritten shapes interfere with one another in the way eal leaves displace one another on a live plant. Seeing the transfer of locational logic with the ddition of dimensional information allows us to imagine similar transfers with increasingly architectural" material as we build systems up from more abstract, diagrammatic armatures. Matter drives organization as physics draws the diagram.

Che key here is to accept that one *invents* some material at each step along the way—that it can ever be found entirely in the preceding step. To "rewrite" an underlying armature is not to simply wrap it in a material stand-in (the costume of building materials on the diagrammatic body underneath) but rather to progressively erase and redraw the diagram through substance (this works only when the substance corresponds to some material, buildable reality). Hence, the increasingly intelligent, physical, and alluring forms we are starting to see in parametric design as in su11's *Dune House*, where a parametric armature becomes structure, realistic in material, dimension, and disposition. With this material, the hurdle of inflection has been cleared. I sincerely think of this as a milestone in the application of complexity to architecture.

We now confront the higher aspiration of *complexion*, or the full identity of a thing. Deriving from a medieval idea that bodies are the expression of four fundamental "humors"(choleric, melancholic, phlegmatic, sanguine) complexion ultimately involves physiological disposition. Entire, well-formed and functional bodies are what is at stake with this term—no longer homogeneous, self-similar assemblies of parts that cannot possibly address all of the issues involved in whole buildings. This requires real combination of truly disparate systems and so far, with parametric design, we admittedly don't have much of that. Instead we see beds of inflected matter, primed but not yet fired. The interest in taste and temperament is not an attempt to sidestep history and theory in exchange for a consumable "liteness," but a commitment to make sense and product of work that stands among the important developments in recent architectural experimentation.

In 1929 Bataille made a new dictionary entry for the term "formless" in an effort to "bring things down in the world."[2] Parametric design finds itself in a rather awkward position today vis-à-vis this kind of materialism. For me the choice is clear: the *task* of the form is most important, not its meaning...we *all* want the continuity promised by complexity,

out some have yet to understand that real continuity often goes unseen. It is not always expressed at the outermost, visible skin of a thing, but is often found flowing invisibly through it. Only by looking at the *workings* of a structure can its continuity be accurately assessed. Complexion, then, is the resultant amalgam of qualities thrown off of such working bodies. But to get back to your question about component-based surfaces: the roots of this technique lie in complexity theory; specifically, the necessity for huge numbers of components to work interactively to produce large fields of inflected material. This is both a remarkably simple, beautiful idea and an arduous, time-consuming task. The past several years have been consumed largely by the single-minded pursuit of this principle as it applies to architecture, albeit in a rather narrow sense. Seeing the results *and understanding them as provisional,* we now must challenge the necessity for the literal expression of large populations of elements. "Parametric blankets" will inevitably be woven through, buried under, and teased apart as we move toward less literal expressions of population dynamics. I am tired of the complaint "it all looks the same everywhere." Connoisseurs of this work never say this for we know that the idiomatic terrain is variegated even where it seems smooth and that in places, as I've illustrated above, there are deep schisms. And it gets rougher as we go along: the inertia of self-similarity we see today is giving way to increasing difference.

SK: I suppose that for a generation that grew up 'never not' doing architecture in a computer, the etherea of screen-registered lines and surfaces has become the new clay environment, a new type of base matter that can still aspire to nobility through operations. If you are asking the world to wait a bit, how can one deny you this, but the clock does tick…

JP: Important things take years. The variety of experiment and the level of acquired skill is higher today than it has ever been. My main concern is that it feels as good later as it does now.

Payne is referring here to the now well-know phrase of Deleuze to "faire un enfant dans le dos" (to make a baby in/behind one's back) by which he describes the way he sought to use other classical philosophers to produce strange new concepts in the way that a woman can deliberately become pregnant unbeknownst to him. The phrase was famously mistranslated by Brian Massumi as committing "buggery."
4 Georges Bataille, "Formless." *Documents* 7 (December 1929): 382.

Edited by
Tomoko Sakamoto
Albert Ferré
and each of the
contributing offices

Content advisor
Michael Kubo

Design
Reinhard Steger
Actar Pro

Digital production
Carmen Galán
Oriol Rigat

Acknowledgements
Mimi Zeiger
Irene Hwang
Daniel Bosia
Veronika Schmid
Yoshiyuki Hiraiwa
Ayumi Isozaki
Reuben Brambleby
Toby Harling
Christoph Schindler

Printing
Ingoprint SL

ISBN
978-84-96540-79-8

DL
B-326990-08

Printed & bound
in the European Union

Distribution
Actar-D
Roca i Batlle 2
08023 Barcelona
Spain
Tel: +34 93 417 49 93
Fax: +34 93 418 67 07
office@actar-d.com
www.actar-d.com

Actar-D USA
158 Lafayette Street, 5th Fl.
New York
NY 10013
Tel : +1 212-966-2207
Fax : +1 212-966-2214
officeusa@actar-d.com
www.actar-d.com